Threshold

Threshold

Straightforward Answers to Teenagers' Questions About Sex

BY THOMAS MINTZ, M.D. AND LORELIE MILLER MINTZ

ILLUSTRATED BY LORELIE MILLER MINTZ

WALKER AND COMPANY
New York

First published in the United States of America
in 1978 by the Walker Publishing Company, Inc.

Published simultaneously in Canada by Beaverbooks,
Limited, Pickering, Ontario

Trade ISBN: 0-8027-6307-3
Reinf. ISBN: 0-8027-6308-1

Library of Congress Catalog Card Number: 77-78991

Printed in the United States of America

10 9 8 7 6 5 4 3 2 1

To Leslie, Jennifer and Mandy
. . . and the promise of their tomorrow

Contents

Introduction 9

Chapter One   PUBERTY IN GIRLS 11
  Physical Changes   11
  Menstruation   21

Chapter Two   PUBERTY IN BOYS 29
  Physical Changes   29
  Ejaculation   38

Chapter Three   SEXUAL DEVELOPMENT IN GIRLS
                  AND BOYS 45
  Masturbation and Orgasm   45
  Sexual Intercourse   51

Chapter Four   PREGNANCY 57
  Conception   57
  Development   62

Chapter Five   BIRTH 66

Chapter Six   CAUTION AND PRECAUTION 77
  Birth Control   77
  Abortion   83
  Venereal Disease   86

Chapter Seven   FEELINGS 90
  Feelings About the Opposite Sex   90
  Feelings About Your Family   102
  Feelings About Yourself   108

Afterword 115

Index 117

Introduction

YOUR ADOLESCENCE is a very special time in your life. It is the time when your special male or female sexual characteristics begin to develop and when your growth takes its final leap. Adolescence will bring new physical and emotional changes into your life. This physical development is accompanied by changes in how you view yourself, and it is a time in which the world also begins reacting differently to you. The physical development of adolescence will last about five years. Although your emotional and psychological development will continue throughout your life, by the end of adolescence your physical development will have completed itself, and you will be fully grown young men and women.

Adolescence is an exciting and wonderful time of your life. But because so many important changes occur, both physically and emotionally, it is also a time that can bring new anxieties and worries. Many young people going through adolescence, despite their excitement and pride, suffer enormous doubts and uncertainties about themselves and the world around them.

This is one of the main reasons for this book. For while all young people pass over the threshold of adolescence into adulthood having lots of questions and confusing feelings about what is happening to them, most feel very much alone with these feelings. All young people—even those you think wouldn't have a qualm or a question in the world—usually have something about which they feel anxious or confused.

In this book we discuss what you can expect to happen to you physically and emotionally during adolescence and the kinds of questions that most girls and boys have about themselves and about each other. It is usually embarrassing for young people to talk about these subjects with each other, but it is very helpful to understand what the opposite sex experiences and feels.

While many of you will share similar thoughts and feelings, your experience with puberty will be a very personal and special one—which only you can feel! And you will have many kinds of feelings. You will feel joy and you will feel pain, fervent hopes and keen disappointment, discovery and pride amidst old fears, intense new friendships and lonely isolation, certainty and security laced with confusion and doubt.

It is our hope that by reading this book your personal journey over the threshold of adolescence will be a more understandable and therefore a happier one.

CHAPTER ONE

Puberty in Girls

PHYSICAL CHANGES

Puberty is the word for the physical changes that occur during adolescence. As a general rule, most girls begin their sexual maturation sooner than boys. You may begin to notice this when a lot of the boys around you suddenly begin to look smaller and shorter than they were! Of course they are not getting shorter—you are starting your growth spurt of puberty and are getting taller. In a few years' time, when boys begin their sexual maturation, most of them will not only catch up but might outdistance you in height.

You may also notice that not all the girls are growing taller as suddenly as you are. Not only do people go through adolescent development at different times but the characteristics that make people look different begin to show up. Some people are destined to be short. Others are destined to be taller. Some girls will be small-breasted, others larger. Different bodies for different people.

Your first sign of puberty will be when your nipples become enlarged and begin to bud. Soon after, breast tissue will begin to fill out, and your breasts will begin to have a rounder, fuller shape. Around this time, hair under your arms and around your pubic area will begin to develop. The reproductive organs inside your body will begin to develop in preparation for the menstrual periods, which will occur later on in your adolescence.

Some parts of your female sexual anatomy are difficult to

11

see. Because of this, exactly what and where your sexual parts are can seem like a big mystery. But you can easily become familiar with all the outside sexual parts you have. Using a hand mirror to look at your female genitals (another word for the sexual parts of your body) makes this an easy learning process.

Here is what you will see:

- The clitoris is located first, near the front side of your body. The clitoris, a little round bump of extremely sensitive tissue, responds with much sensation to even a little stimulation.

- The urethra is a tiny opening just behind the clitoris. This is where urine comes out.

EXTERNAL FEMALE GENITALS

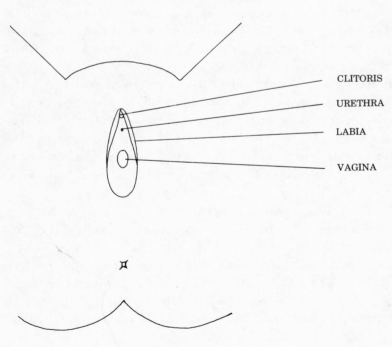

CLITORIS

URETHRA

LABIA

VAGINA

• The vagina is the larger opening, right in the middle. The vagina serves many functions. It is the place where the fluid of menstruation seeps out during a woman's period. In childbirth, the vagina stretches wide to allow a baby to be born. The vagina, although not as sensitive to sexual sensations as the clitoris, is also where the penis is inserted during sexual intercourse.

• The skin folds that surround your female genitals are called the labia.

• Sometimes the opening of the vagina is covered by a very fragile, thin-skin membrane called a hymen. Sometimes there is no membrane at all. It does not mean anything is wrong if you have, or have not, a hymen. Both situations are normal.

• Toward the back of your body is the rectal opening. This opening is in the same place in both males and females.

Inside your body, not visible to you, are your reproductive organs:

• The inside of your vagina leads, like an elastic tube, up to the opening of the uterus. The opening of the uterus is closed tightly, like the drawstrings of a purse. This closed area is called the cervix. During menstruation the cervix opens a very tiny bit to allow the menstrual blood to seep out. During childbirth the cervix stretches wide open to allow a baby to move from the uterus, down the vagina, and to slide out into the world. The uterus itself is a pear-shaped, hollow organ.

• At each side of the uterus you have an ovary and a fallopian tube. Your ovaries are stocked with about half a million tiny eggs. Thousands of these eggs could fit on the head of a pin. If one of these eggs were to someday be fertilized by a male sperm, another life would begin—your baby.

• The fallopian tubes are hollow tubes that act as roads for the eggs to travel upon during the menstrual cycle. At the proper time in each cycle usually only one egg at a time will be released from one of the ovaries and will be guided toward the uterus by the fallopian tubes.

FEMALE INTERNAL REPRODUCTIVE ORGANS

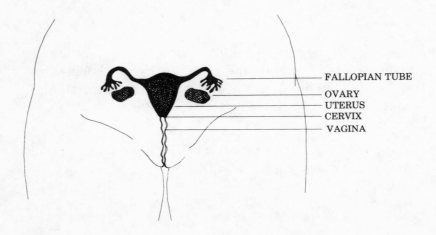

FALLOPIAN TUBE

OVARY
UTERUS
CERVIX
VAGINA

Does anything ever come out of the clitoris?

Nothing ever comes out of the clitoris. It is a very sensitive sexual part of your body and has no other function. This area of your body provides you with a great deal of pleasure as you grow older. The sensitive clitoris is made of the same kind of tissue—called erectile tissue—as the penis is.

How far up into the body does the vagina go?

It goes up into the body at a slight backward angle for about three to four inches when you are finally mature.

What is inside the vagina?

The vagina has nothing in it. It is lined with moist skin that is able to expand easily. The skin feels soft, like the inside of your cheek.

Do smaller women have smaller vaginas and bigger women bigger ones?

No. The size of women's vaginas is pretty similar and has no relation to their body size. The size of the vagina is not really one fixed size. It is expandable to different sizes.

Does anything come out of the vagina except for menstruation?

Not really. A drop or two of vaginal discharge may be noticeable to you occasionally. Secretions keep the vagina clean and healthy.

Does the uterus grow during puberty?

Yes. It reaches adult size at the end of your adolescent development. This size is about the same as that of a closed fist. By that time, it will also have attained the ability to function as the home of a baby during pregnancy.

Can you feel your ovaries or uterus or fallopian tubes from the outside?

You cannot feel them from the outside, though a person who has been properly trained can during a special female pelvic medical examination.

Can pubic hair be a different color than the hair on your head?

Yes. While pubic hair is usually somewhat the same color, it is often many shades darker than the hair on your head. For example, if you have blond or red hair, while your pubic hair may show many of the same tones, it can be many shades darker, so that a difference is apparent.

I am taller than the girls and boys I know. Will I always be taller than everyone?

No. You may always be taller than some people, maybe even a lot of people—especially if your parents and grandparents were tall too—but you will not be taller than everyone. The height of your parents is about the best predictor of how tall you will be. In puberty, people grow at such different rates that it is very difficult to tell who will end up where. Some shoot up early but end being shorter than others who start later on. It is hard to be the tallest girl—especially when some people still have the mistaken notion that girls have to be the short ones.

I am taller and bigger than a lot of girls and boys I know, and it feels very "unfeminine." Why is it that the small, tiny girls seem more feminine?

This is a hand-me-down fairy tale from the days when men were supposed to be as big, strong, and powerful as ape-men. Naturally this ideal was a lot easier to achieve if women were tiny, dainty, and helpless. Being "feminine" is a state of mind, not a state of size. Being "feminine" no longer has to have anything to do with being petite and dainty (and helpless). Time, of course, will solve much of this height difference as those around you catch up. In the meantime it will help your self-image if you make sure you are not overweight and if you try to rethink what *feminine* means to you and why. You may change your opinion of yourself by a new definition for that word.

What does feminine *mean?*

It is just a label used to describe female gender, though it sometimes carries with it stereotyped images. You can be feminine if you play soccer, basketball, and football. You can be feminine if you like to sew, cook, and do needlepoint. All girls are feminine in their own way, and these ways may change as you do.

When will I stop growing?

Anywhere from about fifteen to seventeen years of age your physical growth will slow down and eventually stop.

I am beginning to develop hair and breasts, and no one else I know has. Can it be stopped or slowed down?

No. Puberty is just coming earlier for you than it is for your friends. It can be very hard for a girl to begin her sexual maturation sooner than other girls around her, because it brings feelings of being painfully different—different from the way you were before and different from everyone else as well. Other youngsters, not knowing how to respond to obvious changes such as breast development, may not always be kind. Sooner, much sooner than you realize, others around you will begin their adolescent development, and you won't feel so embarrassed about your own.

At what age do breasts begin to grow?

There is no exact age for breast development to begin, just as there is no exact age for puberty to begin. Breast development usually begins at about the same time pubic hair begins to develop, anywhere from ages ten to fifteen—and usually around eleven or twelve.

My nipples look different than they used to, but I don't have any breasts. What is happening to them?

The first sign of breast development is the enlargement of nipple tissue. Children have nipples that are very flat and small. Before the entire breast begins to develop, the nipples become larger and fuller—swollen looking, getting darker and larger. Gradually breast tissue around the nipples will become fuller.

BREAST DEVELOPMENT

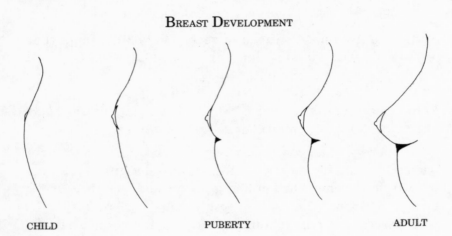

CHILD   PUBERTY   ADULT

How can I tell what size my breasts will be?

Every female will develop breast tissue, but it is difficult to know how much. If all or most of your female relatives are small-breasted, the chances are that you will be small-breasted too, and the opposite is also true. Each has its own advantages.

My nipples are darker and larger than other girls I see. Theirs are smaller and pinker. Why?

This means you probably have a darker complexion and darker hair. It is normal for nipples to vary somewhat depending upon skin color. Fair-skinned, light-haired girls may have lighter tissue. Darker girls have darker tissue. In all adult females the nipples will darken after the first child is born.

I have very large breasts, and hardly anyone I know has any breasts at all. I feel embarrassed about this. Is there anything I can do to make them smaller?

At this stage in your life, full breasts can cause you to feel painfully and embarrassingly different from other girls who may not have developed yet. Nothing practical can make your breasts smaller except wearing clothes that do not emphasize them. Beginning your physical development earlier or having large breasts before others have any can feel strange and new. Give yourself time to get used to your figure. Soon, when those around you start their own breast development, you will not feel embarrassed, even though your breasts may always be larger than those of many girls you know. You may find some of your tiny-breasted friends wishing they were like you. Until then, remind yourself that you will soon consider your natural development quite beautiful.

My breasts are so small that I'm almost perfectly flat-chested. Girls the same age and size as me all seem to have bigger breasts. Is there anything I can do to grow bigger breasts?

If you have already been having menstrual periods for quite some time, the chances are that your breasts will only get a little larger. There is really nothing you can do to make them grow larger. If you have not yet menstruated or have only just started you probably have not reached your full breast development, and there will be more to come. Some girls develop breasts sooner, and it may seem to you that they will always have larger breasts than you. If you do end up small-breasted, chances are that it goes best with your type of figure. Also, being smaller breasted means being free of the necessity to wear a constricting brassiere. You will have a freedom of choice that many girls with large breasts (which may need support) don't have. Most men find small-breasted women are just as attractive as large-breasted women.

Are nipples supposed to be sensitive?

Yes. Nipples are made of erectile tissue. This is the same kind of tissue other sexually sensitive areas of the body are made of, such as the clitoris in the female and the penis in the male.

Does your waist get smaller when you start getting breasts?

In adolescence, your "figure" begins to develop. As the breasts develop and your hips round out, your waist will appear smaller. You will grow in height and become "curvier."

My breasts look lopsided. Is that normal?

It is very common for one breast to be slightly smaller, larger, higher, or lower than the other. Usually this is quite unnoticeable except under close scrutiny. If you look closely enough in a mirror or at half of a photograph, you will notice that your face is lopsided too. One side of our body does not perfectly match the other, anywhere.

Are boys more attracted to big-breasted girls?

Some are, some are not. Attractiveness is usually based on a combination of personality and physical traits, not just big breasts. Everyone has his or her own particular combination of unique traits. This is what attracts people to each other.

I have sort of small-to-medium breasts, and I don't like to wear a bra. But a lot of boys seem to stare at me, and I feel embarrassed. When should a girl start wearing a bra? Or should she wear one at all?

First of all, it's probably true that the boys will stare even if you do wear a bra! A compromise might help you feel more comfortable for now. Perhaps you could try wearing a bra when you wear especially revealing clothes that are thin or tight and go without a bra at other times when it is less likely to cause you embarrassment. Whether or not you wear a bra should depend upon how comfortable you feel, both physically and emotionally. You might also not be so embarrassed by realizing that "stares" are really just compliments about your developing body.

I am very embarrassed about undressing in front of other girls, even in front of my mother. My friends don't seem embarrassed;

is there something wrong with me? I never used to feel this way.

No. There is nothing wrong with you. Modesty — feelings about wanting to keep your body private — are very common. Getting used to your own body development takes a long time. After you feel more comfortable with the changes that have taken place in you, such as having breasts and pubic hair, it may be easier for you to let other people see you. Also, even though your friends may not show it as much, I would bet that they have some of the same feelings about undressing too. As you get more courage to take a chance, try getting undressed a few times in front of other girls. Experience will help ease some of your embarrassment.

MENSTRUATION

The occurrence of the menstrual cycle is of tremendous importance in your life and can make you feel very grown up and special. It can also make you feel very curious about what is happening to you. Is it happening in the right way and at the right time?

The menstrual cycle begins with the appearance of a bloody fluid, which seeps out of the vagina for anywhere from three to seven days once each month. It signals that your adolescent development has really gotten under way. It tells you that your body is working just as it should, preparing itself to be an adult body capable of bearing children!

At some point during adolescence special female hormones will cause just one of the thousands of eggs within one of your ovaries to ripen. This egg, when ripe, is the size of a particle of dust and will pop out of the ovary and begin its journey down the fallopian tube into the uterus.

While the egg is ripening, your uterus is also doing its work. The uterus will be building up a lining of tissue within — a place where your ripened egg will be nourished in case it is fertilized by a male sperm during its journey. In that case the egg would need the uterine lining for nourishment so that it could begin to develop into a baby.

You, of course, will be the one to decide when you wish to conceive, but your uterus has no way of knowing your future plans. Therefore, each month it prepares its nutrient bed for your egg—just in case.

BEGINNING A MENSTRUATION CYCLE

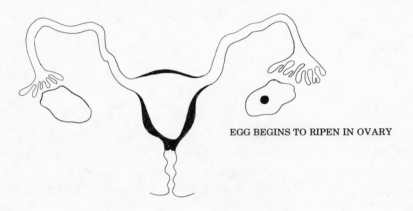

EGG BEGINS TO RIPEN IN OVARY

MIDWAY THROUGH A MENSTRUATION CYCLE

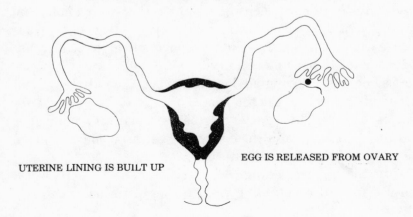

UTERINE LINING IS BUILT UP   EGG IS RELEASED FROM OVARY

END OF MENSTRUATION CYCLE A MENSTRUATION PERIOD

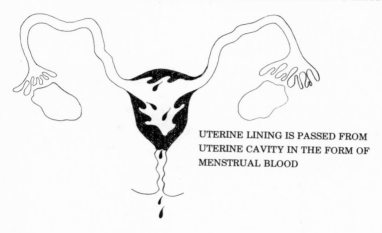

UTERINE LINING IS PASSED FROM
UTERINE CAVITY IN THE FORM OF
MENSTRUAL BLOOD

If the egg is not fertilized, it has no use for the lining of tissue and blood within the uterus. So, once the unfertilized egg has completed its journey into the uterus this lining will slowly seep out of the uterus and down the vagina in the form of a menstrual period. This entire process is repeated each and every month. Each month your ovaries will release just one ripened egg, and each month your uterus will again build up a new lining of tissue—just in case. Each month, after the un-fertilized egg finishes its journey, another menstrual period will occur.

This cycle is only stopped when a pregnancy occurs. The egg, now a fertilized one, buries itself in the lining of tissue within the uterus and begins to develop into a baby. For the entire length of the pregnancy there will be no menstrual periods. Then, sometime after the birth of the baby, the menstrual cycle will resume.

At what age do periods start?

Menstrual periods can begin anywhere from age ten to age sixteen. Many begin between twelve and thirteen. The time you start to menstruate has nothing at all to do with your later ability to have children. It does not affect your adolescent development either. Each body has its own special built-in timetable.

What starts menstruation?

Your master gland, the pituitary, begins to secrete special hormones during the adolescent years. The presence of these hormones in turn signals the production of special female hormones. The balance of these special female hormones triggers the release of the uterine lining and blood each month.

Does everyone menstruate?

Yes. All girls, sooner or later, at some time between the ages of ten and sixteen (unless there is a rare medical condition), will begin to menstruate.

Does it hurt to menstruate?

Even though the idea of "bleeding" may seem painful, periods are usually not painful at all. At first, because it is a new and unusual event, there may be some tightness about your lower abdominal muscles. Some girls complain of a sensation of fullness or dull aching in the lower abdomen or lower back. Menstrual periods as a rule, however, are not painful. The discomfort, called menstrual cramps, can usually be helped by aspirin or relaxation. Often, any cramps that do appear only last for the first day or two at most. Most women are able to go about their regular activities without any trouble at all during their periods.

Do you bleed a lot during menstruation?

No. It may seem like a lot, but actually it is only a very, very, slight amount—a few ounces at most. "Bleeding" every month can sound more scary than it really is. The blood does not pour out of you, and it does not mean that anything is wrong. Menstruation is a sign that your body is doing exactly what it is supposed to be doing.

Why does the idea of menstruation scare me?

Menstrual periods can have an element of fright in them because the sight of blood is alarming to most people, and the thought of bleeding from your vagina can be frightening. It is helpful to remember that your periods are not the same kind of blood that comes from being hurt or injured. Usually, once you have menstruated a few times and are used to the regular way in which it starts and stops, you will begin to feel much more natural and comfortable with the process. It will also be comforting for you if you learn about menstruation beforehand. Talk about it with your mother or sister or father or a friend. And remind yourself that it is a natural thing your body is supposed to do. Growing up is always a little scary—to everyone.

Can you bleed so much that you can get sick?

No. Menstruation is not like losing blood from an injury. You only lose a very small amount, and it is being discarded from your body as unnecessary. Menstruation is the way your uterus "cleans house." An adequate diet easily replenishes any lost blood.

Can you tell when you are going to get your period, especially a first period?

Usually it is hard to know when your first period will arrive. A good rule is to expect your period at least a full year after your breasts and body hair begin to develop. Once periods do begin, they become more regular, coming each month at approximately the same date, anywhere from twenty-eight to thirty-one days apart. In the beginning, however, for a year or so, your periods may be irregular and missing months is common.

What if I get my period at school? or away from home?

Usually any grown-up man or woman is very good at helping young girls deal with these situations. You will have plenty of time to go to the nurse's office at school or to the bathroom and put on a sanitary napkin. Don't panic. It will help if you talk to your mother about this before your periods begin, or just plan it out in your own mind. But, even if you don't know exactly what to do, it is very easy to learn, and help is always available from any adult nearby.

Can people tell when you are having a period?

Not unless you tell them yourself. Often young girls are very embarrassed or worried about having other people know. Sometimes it can seem that when something important happens to you, especially something as intimate as having a period, the whole world knows. While this is indeed a private matter, you can be assured it always remains a private matter, not visible or obvious to anyone else in any way.

Does menstruation make you look different?

Menstruation doesn't change your looks. However, as a sign of your entire physical development, you do look different. Your figure becomes more developed and taller; breast development is obvious; and your facial features begin to take on more adult contours.

Does menstruation affect your personality at all?

Menstruation only affects your personality by its effect on you emotionally. Menstruation can make you feel excited about life and about being on the way to becoming a grown-up.

Can you have a baby as soon as you have had your first period?

Menstruation means that your body is *becoming* able to have a baby. It usually takes anywhere from one to three years after your periods have begun to develop that ability completely.

What is a douche? Is it something to use after you start menstruation?

A douche is a special way of washing the inside of the vagina, but this is not ever necessary, even after periods. Vaginal secretions keep the vagina clean and healthy. Normal soap-and-water washing can clean the external genitals, and the internal secretions take care of the rest.

Can you go swimming while you menstruate?

Yes. This is easily possible once you are able to use internal sanitary napkins, such as tampons. Swimming will not hurt you at all. You can play tennis, go horseback riding, do anything you feel comfortable doing.

Does menstruation make you break out in pimples?

Menstruation itself does not cause pimples. During adolescence, the very same hormones that cause your sexual development sometimes cause excess oil to be produced by your skin glands. This excess oil production may occur at the time of your periods. Accumulation of this oil upon your skin results in clogging of the pores, and this can cause pimples. You can keep your skin pores from becoming clogged by washing with soap and water.

No one else I know menstruates except me, and it is very embarrassing. Is there any way to make periods stop or to prevent them?

No doctor would give you medication to stop your periods.

Menstruation is a drastic change from the earlier days of childhood. It can make you feel terribly different. Try to remind yourself that all girls, sooner or later, will begin to menstruate, and then you won't feel so unusual.

My girl friend only barely menstruates for two days, and I seem to have a very heavy period for a whole week. Is something wrong with me?

Not at all. The length of time of menstrual periods varies among different women. Some menstruate from three to four days, others six to seven, and others anywhere in between. The amount of fluid in menstrual periods differs a small amount, which causes variation in the duration of periods. "More blood" is just as healthy as "less blood."

Is it okay for girls to use Tampax when they get their period?

The external sanitary napkin, sometimes called a Modess or a Kotex, is best used in the very beginning. After the periods have become somewhat established, an internal sanitary napkin, or tampon, can be used. Using a tampon does not change the state of "virginity." Even women and girls who have not had sexual intercourse can use them. Junior-sized tampons are available and easy to use. There are simple instructions in the package for you to follow. An older sister, mother, or even more experienced friends can help you learn how to use it. Also a gynecologist—a doctor who specializes in treating women and their sex organs—can be very helpful in instructing you and in answering any questions you may have.

Do you have menstrual periods forever?

No. Although this probably will seem like forever, you will have them until you are approximately fifty or older. Then you will undergo what is called the menopause. This is the reverse process of adolescence, when your periods begin to stop.

CHAPTER TWO

Puberty in Boys

PHYSICAL CHANGES

Because you are boys, some of you are destined to be taller than your female sisters. You will have more body hair, facial hair, a deeper voice, and more muscular development. You will, however, not start your adolescent development until about two years after girls start theirs. It is not uncommon to see some of the girls you know begin suddenly to outdistance you in height somewhere around your eleventh year. Later on, when your adolescent development has begun, it is most likely that you will not only soon catch up but surpass in height most of the girls you know. No matter who starts or stops first, it all evens out very satisfactorily in the end.

A boy's sexual organ, the penis, is accompanied by two male glands called testicles. These testicles are inside a loose sac of skin, called the scrotum. Inside the body another male gland, called the prostate, is located. Along with other physical growth and development during adolescence, these sexual organs will begin to increase in size, to give new feelings, and to function in different ways than they did in childhood.

Early adolescence is announced by the appearance of downy hair growth around your penis. This is accompanied by a slight increase in the size of your penis and testicles. You may notice that the skin that surrounds your testicles is becoming a bit coarser and redder. Hair will begin to appear under your arms too.

Uncircumcised Penis

————— FORESKIN

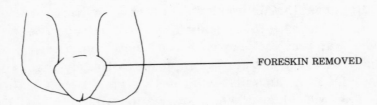

Circumcised Penis

————— FORESKIN REMOVED

Later on, during the middle portion of your adolescence, the pubic hair surrounding your penis will become denser and coarser, and the hair under your arms will thicken. As your penis and testicles continue growing, you will begin to man-ufacture sperm and develop the ability to ejaculate (release) sperm fluid. This experience will be associated with very pleasurable sensations and will mark the beginning of your capacity to father children.

About the middle of your adolescence, you will notice that your voice may begin to crackle at odd times. It is in the process of becoming lower. It will continue to become lower and more stable toward the end of your adolescent years.

Late adolescence brings the appearance of facial and chest hair. Your testicles and penis will complete their growth and reproductive ability. Your rate of growth in height will begin to decline, but your muscular development, along with facial and body hair growth, will continue for an additional few years.

At the end of your adolescence, your strength will have approximately doubled, your beard will be almost full, and you will have reached your full growth as a sexually developed young man.

How old will I be when adolescence starts?

Most boys begin adolescent development somewhere around twelve years of age. Others may begin earlier, and still others not until they are fifteen or even sixteen.

What if I am in my late teens and still don't have any of the signs of adolescence?

It will just mean that your adolescent development will start a bit later than other boys you may know. Just have patience. All boys grow into manhood, even though this may sometimes seem impossible.

Do you start to grow taller right at the beginning of adolescence?

Yes. One of the very first things you may notice is that you are getting taller. At this point in your life getting taller is still equated with getting older. As you get older, feeling grown-up will not depend on your height. At the beginning of adolescence, growing is a bit like watching a kettle and waiting for the water to boil—it seems to take forever.

Is there anything I can do to make myself taller?

Not really. Your rate of growth, and limit of growth, are a

preset part of your inheritance. Even though height is inherited from parents, it is true that each generation is a bit taller than their parent generation. Good health and nutrition are producing taller people. If a grandfather, father, and full-grown son were to stand in a row, it is probable that the youngest son would be tallest. In childhood being tallest is like being oldest, strongest, and most powerful, like our parents. You will later discover that this is not true at all. Feeling strong, powerful, and grown-up will depend less and less upon how tall you are. But along the way, good posture can make the most of every inch you have!

Both my parents are tall, and my brother and sister are tall. Why am I still the shortest even though I'm not the youngest?

It is sometimes difficult to give up the taller position in a family to a younger brother or sister. Often younger siblings catch up and grow taller than their once-bigger brothers or sisters. People grow at such different rates, however, that it is difficult to tell who will end up taller until everyone has completed his or her adolescence. Your younger siblings may have started their growth spurt before you have, or you may in fact end up not quite as tall. Being the shortest in a family can make it seem that you are shorter than everyone in the whole world. But you can be tall in personal stature without being physically tall. In adulthood what makes people feel tall is not how they measure up in feet and inches but how they feel about themselves as people—what they can do and what they can accomplish.

My older brother says he was bigger than me at my age. He is a lot bigger than me now. Does that mean he will always be bigger?

No. He may want to be bigger always, but height can vary between brothers, and age has nothing to do with who ends up taller. He will always be older than you but not necessarily bigger. Even if he were, "bigger" does not mean the same as "better," and "smaller" does not mean the same as "not as good as."

Does the penis only grow in adolescence?

No. It grows slightly during childhood. The major growth, however, takes place during adolescence. Your penis, your testicles, and even the skin of your testicles will all grow and change. The penis becomes thicker and longer, the testicles larger, and the skin rougher and darker. All this happens gradually. The penis stops growing at the end of adolescence.

When will my penis start to grow?

It will grow at the beginning of adolescence. You will notice that your penis is very gradually beginning to change and to grow, along with the rest of you.

If you are short, or have small hands or feet, does that mean you will have a small penis?

No. There is no "sign" that tells how big or how small a male's penis is or will be. Penis size has nothing to do with how tall or how short a man is—or what size shoes he wears. Size of any sort has nothing to do with how masculine you will be or feel or what kind of man you will be.

Why do some boys have a penis that looks bigger than mine even though they are smaller than me?

One of the reasons is that body size has nothing to do with penis size. And penis size does vary a little bit from one person to another. Second of all, other boys may have begun their adolescent development before you. Their penises may have already begun to grow and develop whereas yours may not.

Is the size of a penis important? I hear my brother and his friends always talking about this.

Many young boys, and sometimes even grown men, have the mistaken notion that penis size means something special. Because there is so much feeling and pleasure centered on the penis, some males equate the size of their penis with the size of their masculinity or ability to have pleasure from sex. Nothing could be further from the truth. It does not make anyone any stronger, smarter, braver, or better to have a slightly larger penis. When you are grown, and make love to a woman, a slightly larger penis size will not in itself make you a good lover or give you any more pleasure.

Are adult penises all the same size?

Penis size is roughly the same in grown men, although size can vary slightly. Differences in penis size are most noticeable when the penis is soft. In the erect position, most adult penises are generally the same size.

When does the penis stop growing?

At the end of adolescence, anywhere from ages seventeen to twenty-one, sexual development and your growth in height will be complete. Your beard and muscle growth, however, still continue for a few years longer.

Why do some boys have a skin covering over the end of their penis?

Boys who have skin covering the tip of their penis are un-circumcised, and the skin covering is called a foreskin. Boys who have no foreskin have been circumcised, which means that the foreskin was surgically removed at birth. Some people prefer to leave the foreskin on the tip of the penis, others prefer to have it removed at birth. It does not at all affect the size or function either way. It is simply a cultural preference.

Sometimes I worry about my penis getting hurt or falling off or shrinking. Does this ever happen?

This kind of worry is common among boys and even among some men. The penis, being a very sensitive organ, is something that you feel the need to protect. The fear of losing or hurting your penis or having it shrink is just an unnecessary anxiety. Most males do not worry about their arms or legs getting hurt or falling off, because their arms or legs do not mean as much to their "maleness" as their penis does. The reality is that your penis will not get hurt, nor will it shrink or ever fall off. If you understand the reasons behind this worry, it will gradually lessen.

Do all boys grow hair on their face?

Yes. Some men have a very slight beard; others have a thick and coarse beard. Facial hair is totally absent only in unusual medical conditions. Hair will usually first appear above your upper lip.

How old will I be when I have to start shaving?

This will depend upon just how thick and heavy your facial hair is and when you begin to grow it. In early teens, it is very unusual to have to shave. Hair growth on the face starts after other adolescent development, and it is very fine hair at first. You may have a very slight or fine beard, or you may have very dark, coarse hair that needs shaving before it is even fully grown. And of course, you may like the idea of shaving before you need to shave, which is okay too.

Does shaving hair make it grow faster?

No. Shaving will not make you develop a beard any faster than your body is programmed to make it grow.

Does growing hair on your face make you get pimples?

No. Teen-age acne is a result of the excess oil produced by skin glands. This excess oil production is triggered by the increased sex hormones circulating in your body during adolescence. When the oil becomes clogged in skin pores, pimples can develop. Try to keep your hair washed frequently and your hands and face clean to avoid excess oil building up on your skin.

How can I tell if I will ever get bald when I grow up?

You really can't tell except by studying very closely all the photo albums of all your family ancestors. Then you might make a good guess—but still only a guess.

If you have a lot of facial hair does it mean you won't get bald?

No. The amount of facial hair growth has nothing to do with baldness. Many men with thick, coarse beards may be bald; others with very slight fine beards may not be. The pattern for baldness or no baldness lies in the genes you've inherited. Losing hair in adulthood doesn't mean you lose any of your "maleness." Men are every bit as masculine with less hair.

Do all boys' voices change?

Yes. Boys always get lower and deeper voices as they grow and develop. This does not mean that every boy will develop a deep, rich bass or baritone voice, but every boy will have a lower adult voice than his childhood voice, and lower than most female voices.

What makes the voice get lower?

The larynx, your voice box, enlarges during sexual development, and so it makes the sound of your voice resonate a bit lower.

Will my muscles get hard and bigger automatically?

Males normally develop more muscle than females, and your body muscles will increase in size and strength automatically as you grow. Your particular body build will of course depend upon inherited factors. It won't do you any good to wait and wish for a six-foot-five-inch frame if your family characteristics are all on the slight side of five foot ten. Exercise, however, can make muscles larger and harder. Also, no matter what you've inherited, you can become soft and flabby if you overeat and do not exercise.

Do girls like muscular, athletic boys better?

Some do, and some don't. Sometimes a particular physique will attract some girls, but muscles alone are not enough to cement a relationship. For many girls, muscles are not important at all. Usually people who have compatible interests and similar values will find each other interesting and fun to be with. This is what makes someone attractive in a special way.

MALE INTERNAL REPRODUCTIVE ORGANS

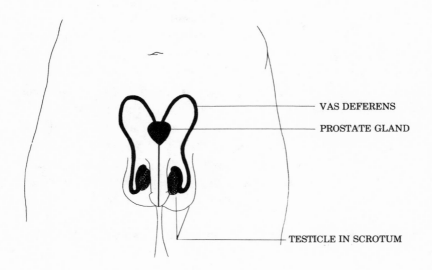

VAS DEFERENS

PROSTATE GLAND

TESTICLE IN SCROTUM

What does masculine *mean?*

It is a label used to describe male gender that sometimes carries with it stereotyped images. You can be masculine if you like to cook, cry at sentimental movies, and write poetry. You can be masculine if you play football and baseball and pride yourself about never crying. All boys are masculine in their own way, and as you grow and change, so may your masculinity.

EJACULATION

During the middle of your adolescence, your sexual organs will begin to function differently as they complete their development. The special male sex hormones that your body now begins to manufacture in greater amounts will cause your testicles to begin producing sperm. These same hormones will continue to change the size of your penis and how it feels and functions.

By now you are probably familiar with the physical sensations that make your penis become stiff and erect. This is called an erection. During your early childhood years, physical stimulation of your penis could bring about an erection, but there was no capacity for ejaculation. In adolescence, physical stimulation as well as sexual thoughts will produce an erection. At this period of your life, along with a more sexually intense erection, you will experience your first ejaculation.

Ejaculation is the squirting out of a small amount of white-colored fluid from the opening at the tip of your penis. Urine comes out of this same opening at other times. This fluid, called seminal fluid, or semen, is a mixture of sperm and fluid that has been produced by your internal sexual organs, the testicles and prostate gland.

Ejaculation occurs during times of intense sexual excitement, when the penis is hard and erect. Emotional feelings and physical stimulation combine to produce the ejaculation. This is also called having an orgasm.

The extremely pleasurable set of feelings produced when there is an orgasm marks the beginning of your adult sexuality. It also marks the beginning of your ability to father a child. When the seminal fluid, containing sperm, enters the female vagina during sexual intercourse, sperm in this fluid can combine with an egg from the woman's ovary to produce a baby. Ejaculation is a tremendously exciting and powerful feeling. It is a most significant milestone on your way toward adulthood.

After an ejaculation your penis will gradually become soft again. Your testicles will continue to manufacture sperm. Whenever your sexual feelings become intense enough to produce another erection and ejaculation, new seminal fluid will be released. This ability will continue throughout your adult life.

What makes ejaculation happen?

Far enough along in sexual development, when special hormones have stimulated the production of sperm, an ejaculation can happen. Exciting sexual emotions, usually combined with physical stimulation of the erect penis, will trigger an intensely pleasurable muscular spasm of your sex organs. This is the spasm that pushes the seminal fluid out of the penis and is what we call an ejaculation.

What does the term to come *mean?*

It is another word for orgasm or ejaculation.

Does the size of your penis have anything to do with when you start to ejaculate?

No. Only the change in size from smaller to bigger. This change means that in the near future you will have the ability to ejaculate. The size of your penis does not affect how it feels or how it functions.

How old will I be when I start to ejaculate?

There is no one definite age for everyone. Usually you can expect ejaculation to occur at least one year after you notice an increase in the size of your penis. This can happen anywhere from ages twelve to sixteen, but most likely around fourteen or fifteen. Don't worry if you don't experience this at the same age as some of your friends. Everyone's body has its own special timing.

Do you ever use up all your sperm?

No. Sperm is continually being manufactured. You only use up what your testicles have made, and then your testicles make it again. You do not need to worry about "saving it." Your body will supply you with all you ever need.

How many sperm do I have?

At the time your sexual development will have completed itself, one ejaculation will contain anywhere from 250 million to 450 million sperm.

Is orgasm the only way the sperm come out?

Yes. The sperm are stored in the body, and during sexual excitement the ejaculation acts as a jet-propelling force that pumps the sperm up through the penis, and during intercourse, into the vagina.

If you have had one ejaculation, does that mean everytime you have an erection you'll have another ejaculation?

No. Often you will have erections that do not result in orgasm. Other times you may have erections that, upon physical stimulation, will produce ejaculation. You will have varying degrees of sexual excitement and varying degrees of erections. Not all erections lead to orgasm.

MALE SPERM

What if I don't ever have an ejaculation?

There is no real possibility of this. Your body will accomplish this for you, in its own good time. Sooner or later you will experience ejaculation unless a very rare condition exists where medical treatment is necessary.

Can you get a girl pregnant the first time you ejaculate?

No. It takes anywhere from one to three years for boys (and girls too) to develop fully their ability to produce children, even though they may have begun to ejaculate or have periods. It's wisest to assume, however, that you do have that power and to take precautions if you have sexual relations with a female.

Does the urine ever get mixed up with the sperm?

No. Special valves inside prevent this. Although the same opening is used for both ejaculation and urination, these two different functions never get in each other's way. When seminal fluid is using the route to your urethra, the urine cannot, and when urine is using the route, ejaculation cannot.

Why do I wake up with an erection?

This is a normal happening. Most men have morning erections all the time but do not consider these the same as erections brought on by specific sexual stimuli.

Why does my penis sometimes get hard when I'm not even thinking about anything?

Erections in adolescence are caused by either of three things: physical stimulation, conscious sexual thoughts, or unconscious sexual thoughts. Even if you are "not thinking about anything in particular," thoughts may be going on in you unconsciously, thoughts you are not aware of, that are sexually stimulating. A shaft of sunlight and its warmth on your penis or a fold of clothing can even cause physical stimulation you are unaware of. These "uncontrollable" erections are a normal part of development and happen to every male.

Sometimes I get an erection at an embarrassing moment. How can I make it go away?

The best thing is to try not to dwell on it and just wait. If you relax emotionally, in a while your penis and the rest of your body will do the same. As you get older, you will be less susceptible and more able to control these erections.

I worry about not having enough erections.

Even an occasional erection shows that your sexual organs are working. You will have as many erections as your particular mind and body want and need. Your sexual development does not depend on how many erections you get.

My friend is one year younger than me and says he can ejaculate, but I never have. Why?

Some boys develop at an earlier age than others do. Everyone has a different timing to his or her sexual development. Ejaculating at a younger age has no effect upon how you develop into an adult male.

Are ejaculations bad for you?

No. Having an ejaculation and orgasm is a normal part of your sexual functioning. It will not stop your growth, sap your strength (except for a few minutes afterward), or hurt you in any way. People who felt guilty about the thoughts surrounding their sexual arousal and orgasm were sure they would be punished, so they developed all sorts of reasons why sexual activities must be curbed. But these are all myths. Ejaculations are not bad for you.

Some boys say they come three times in a row, and I can't. Is something wrong with me?

No. Usually some rest period is necessary before sexual excitement builds to the point where another erection and ejaculation occurs. Most of the time natural interests in other aspects of life will give the body plenty of time to rest before another time of sexual excitement. Some boys brag a lot about their sexual abilities and activities—real or imaginary—because they think it makes them seem more masculine. What it really does is show how insecure they really feel. Don't worry if you never have more than one ejaculation at a time. That is normal.

What is a wet dream?

At some point during your adolescence you may wake up and

find your sheets, penis, or pajamas wet with a bit of sticky fluid. This means that you have had an erection and ejaculation in your sleep! Dreams and thoughts during sleep can cause the same kind of sexual excitement as when awake. Wet dreams are very common among boys and men and are nothing to worry about. The "wetness" of your dream and of your sheets has no connection to the bed-wetting of very young children.

One of my testicles is higher than the other.

It is normal for the left testicle to hang a bit lower than the right.

CHAPTER THREE

Sexual Development
in Girls and Boys

MASTURBATION AND ORGASM

As your body begins its sexual development, it is natural and normal to have increased feelings, thoughts, and questions of a purely sexual nature.

Boys' sexual feelings, and experiences are closely tied in with the reproductive function. Ejaculation, the ability to ejaculate sperm, is a sexually pleasurable experience for boys.

In girls, sexually pleasurable feelings are not as closely tied to the reproductive function. Many girls may experience the sexually pleasurable feelings of orgasm before they have menstrual periods or perhaps later on in development. In females, sexual feelings and sexual pleasure are very independent of the ability to reproduce.

Aside from this difference, the development of increasingly pleasurable sexual feelings for both sexes takes place gradually during adolescence. One of the most common ways in which sexual feelings begin to show themselves is through masturbation.

Many young children, even infants, instinctively rub their genitals. Boys rub their penis, the girls their clitoris and genital area simply because it feels good. This is called masturbation.

During adolescence (and even before), masturbation is a way of teaching yourself about how the sexual parts of your body work and feel. During your adolescent development, your increasing sexual feelings and needs will perhaps be satisfied some of the time through masturbation.

Masturbation will usually bring about your first experience with the physical climax of sexual excitement called orgasm. Usually these personal feelings and responses are first experienced alone. Later on in life your sexual feelings will reach out and involve a partner.

Another way sexual feelings begin to show themselves during adolescence is by the "sexual fantasies" that occur, that is, thoughts of a sexual nature. You may weave imaginary stories involving sex, using as the cast of characters your friends, imaginary people, parents, even brothers or sisters. Increased feelings and thoughts about sex can be very embarrassing, confusing, and even frightening when you are young. Very often the guilt many adolescents feel about masturbating is really guilt about having these kinds of thoughts. All thoughts that cause sexual arousal are part of your growing up and discovering the sexual side of your personality. Almost everyone has them (whether they admit it or not—even to themselves), and everyone has all kinds of fantasies. Even the kind you may feel most guilty about!

The development of the sexual side of your personality comes about gradually. Masturbation, sexual fantasies, and the experience of orgasm will come at different times for different people. Some experience these early in growing up, still others not until adulthood. Everyone has his or her own special timing, and no one time is right for everyone.

What makes you have an orgasm?

At some point in your physical growth you will develop the capacity for a sexual orgasm. An orgasm is a very intense and pleasurable muscular spasm and release that happens only when your genitals are physically stimulated and your sexual emotions very aroused. During masturbation, sexual fantasies play an important role in arousing these emotions until orgasm is possible. The combination of physical stimulation and emotional arousal raises sexual excitement to the point where your body triggers this physical climax called orgasm.

What does an orgasm feel like?

Orgasm is often described as a very pleasurable, powerfully strong, throbbing or pulsating feeling centered in the genitals, the warmth of which extends itself to the entire pelvic area. The entire body has some reaction to this sexual state of excitement. The heart beats faster, respiration is increased, the skin becomes flushed, and the nipples become more erect. It is a powerful surge of sexual release that is both emotionally and physically very satisfying.

Can you tell for sure that you have had an orgasm?

If you are afraid of masturbation or the intense sexual excitement aroused, you might not clearly know if an orgasm has occurred, but this is very unusual. Time and experience with these feelings, however, make it very clear that it is an orgasm. If you expect the world to shake and the buildings to rumble, that will not happen during orgasm—unless there is an earthquake. Orgasm, because it occurs when sexual excitement is at such a peak, brings the sudden and dramatic relief that only orgasm can, and as such it will be very obvious, though it may feel like less or more than you imagined.

How long does an orgasm last?

The peak of orgasm lasts about half a minute or so. It is such a powerful feeling that it seems to last longer than it really does.

Does everyone have sexual thoughts?

Yes—to some extent. Sexual fantasies are very normal and necessary in the development of personal sexuality. Some people, however, may be so embarrassed at having these thoughts or by the feelings that they arouse, that they quickly turn them off. Later on, when they are older and do not need to avoid these sensations, they may be more tolerant of their fantasies.

Does everybody masturbate?

No. Many people do, and most people, at some point during their lives, have! But not everyone masturbates. Some people feel scared or guilty and just cannot overcome these feelings to the point where masturbation can be an enjoyable feeling.

Does everybody have an orgasm when he or she masturbates?

No. Boys do not reach full orgasm until they are old enough to experience ejaculation, even though they may have masturbated earlier. Many girls do not always reach orgasm when they masturbate. As you grow toward adulthood and as your sexual development progresses, masturbation will begin to produce orgasm, although not necessarily all of the time. Usually by early adulthood, masturbation will result in orgasm if you want it to, most all of the time.

Do girls and boys have the same kind of orgasm?

It may seem that because girls and boys look so different, their sexual experiences will feel different. But there is really only one difference: Males release seminal fluid in an ejaculation during orgasm, and females do not. Orgasm feels very much the same for both girls and boys.

Can a boy feel like he has had an orgasm even if he hasn't ejaculated?

Not really. Young boys who have not yet begun to ejaculate

may experience a milder form of sexual excitement and have erections, but there is not as great a build-up and release of sexual excitement as there is later on when ejaculation occurs.

What if you only masturbate a little and don't ever have an orgasm? Does that mean something is wrong with you?

Not in the least. Everyone experiences different degrees of sexual feelings from masturbating. Sometimes the sensations lead more quickly to orgasm. Other times people just need to experience these physical sensations and feelings in slower stages. As your body develops, when the timing and situation are right, the sexual climax of orgasm will eventually occur.

What if I'm afraid to masturbate?

First you have to figure out what you are really afraid of and why. It is an emotional reason only you can discover. There is nothing to fear. It is your body and your feelings—they will not harm you. Perhaps you are afraid of what a disapproving parent might think or afraid of these strange, new feelings. You may need to wait until you grow older to want to try this experience. Trying to do something you are not ready for can make you afraid of it.

Can you catch a disease or get sick from masturbation?

Not at all. You will not go crazy, get blind, be sick, or any of the things you may have heard or imagine will happen. Sometimes, guilt and fear over fantasies that occur during masturbation transform themselves into worries about getting sick or having something bad happen. This is really the punishment the person fears he or she deserves for doing and imagining such forbidden things. The feelings and deeds of masturbation will not hurt you.

Do adults masturbate?

Yes, many do. Grown men and women may masturbate less than some adolescents do because they have the opportunity for sexual satisfaction within their relationships with each other. Even with normal sexual relations however, some adults feel the need to masturbate. This probably will not seem so unusual to you if you realize adults like to do a lot of the same things adolescents do.

Is the feeling of orgasm from masturbation the same as from sexual intercourse?

Yes. Some people feel more emotionally intense feelings when they are involved in a sex act with another person, and so they may describe their orgasm then as being more intense. There is always a different feeling when something is being shared with another. But essentially it is the same physical process.

If I don't like to masturbate, does that mean I won't like sex when I get older?

Not at all. Do not worry about it. It is all right not to masturbate. Many people do not. Give yourself time. What you do not like to do now may not be right for you now. Your feelings about masturbation may change as you get older. Someday, when you feel curious or are ready to explore the sensations the sexual parts of your body can have, you will do so.

I know it's all right to masturbate, but why do I still feel so guilty about it?

Most people feel guilty about masturbating, no matter how many times someone tells them it is a normal thing to do. The reason for this is that they really are not feeling guilty about masturbating but feel guilty over the kind of sexual fantasies they have while they are masturbating. Sexually exciting thoughts are normal and necessary to sexual arousal. Any kind and all kinds.

Why, if I don't feel guilty about masturbating, am I so embarrassed about it?

Sometimes it is hard to tell the difference between embarrassment and guilt. Lots of people are embarrassed by very intimate experiences they have, especially sexually intimate experiences. You are embarrassed partly because you think you are the only one with such thoughts and deeds and partly because you think everyone knows! And they, of course, probably feel very much the same way about themselves.

What should you do if you find yourself wanting to masturbate all the time?

Anything done all the time, leaving no room for other feelings and interests to develop, is not good for your overall personality development. If you seem to be getting obsessed with sex, try to develop other interests. Divert your energy to tennis, group sports, or involvement in other activities that will serve to broaden your personality development. These activities will keep you from dwelling unreasonably upon the new physical sensations you have discovered. It is not unusual or abnormal to think about sex "all the time." One of the roads to adulthood is this sexual one. It is just not the only road, so make sure you try them all.

SEXUAL INTERCOURSE

Just as masturbation is a sexual experience for one person, sexual intercourse is an experience shared by two.

In adulthood, and sometimes even in late adolescence, sexual feelings go beyond the personal experience of masturbation and become part of a personal relationship between two people. Adults involved in a loving and trusting emotional relationship usually include sexual intercourse as an important part of their love. Physically sharing the sexual pleasure their bodies give one another complements the emotional love they share.

During the act of sexual intercourse, the male inserts his

erect penis into the female's vagina. Sexual excitement in the female causes the vagina to become lubricated, making it easy for the penis to penetrate and enter. The friction, created by the movement of the penis against the vagina and the sensitive clitoral area, results in very pleasurable and sexually exciting sensations. This pleasurable sexual tension accumulates to a point that eventually triggers the intensely powerful and satisfying muscular contractions in and around the genital area of both male and female that are called orgasm.

In the beginning, sexual intercourse may be a sexual learning process for two people, just as masturbation was a learning process for one person. It can take time to get used to a two-person sexual arrangement and to learn what pleases each other. In the beginning, both partners may not experience orgasm at the same time, and sometimes one partner may not experience it at all. A close, sharing emotional relationship helps provide both people with what they may need in order to develop a good physical relationship.

What does being a virgin *mean?*

It means someone, male or female, who has never had any sexual intercourse.

How does the man get his penis inside the woman?

While this may seem awkward and difficult to accomplish, it is a natural and somewhat easy procedure. In a comfortable position, usually lying down, the man on top of the woman, the woman opens her legs. The man is then able to gently slide his penis into her vagina. Sometimes it helps if the woman guides the penis with her hand. Lubrication of the vagina makes this even more natural and easy. Other positions can be used, but this is a basic one many people find comfortable and enjoyable.

Does it hurt to have sexual intercourse?

Sexual intercourse can provoke anxiety the first time and as such can add to any physical discomfort. For females who have never had intercourse, it can be a bit painful. The pressure of the penis entering the vaginal opening may cause this. After the first time or so, there will be no physical pain.

Is it true that the woman bleeds the first time she has sexual intercourse?

Not always. If she does, it is only a very little bit. The hymen—the membrane that covers the opening to the vagina—may not yet be broken open in women who have never had intercourse, and its being broken or pushed aside by the penis is what can cause the blood. Many women, however, never experience this bleeding.

Can a vagina be too big or too small for a man's penis?

No. The vagina stretches to fit whatever size is necessary. It can stretch a lot or a little, so it is a perfect size for any penis.

Can the penis ever get hurt or stuck inside a vagina during intercourse?

No. The fear of being hurt is just another way of feeling scared to have intimate contact with another person. There is nothing in a vagina to hurt anyone or to cause a penis to get stuck.

Are people ever scared to have sex with another person?

Yes. There may be many reasons for their anxiety, but most people, especially at first, have these kinds of feelings. Even between loving couples, there is some anxiety. People worry about everything from should they do it, to can they do it, to what if they do it, to how did they do when they did it! It takes time and experience to get used to sharing yourself physically and emotionally. Along with the confidence that time and experience brings, love and trust will greatly lessen all these feelings.

How long does it take to have sexual intercourse?

As long as the two people involved want it to. Usually adults like to make love, kissing and touching each other, for a while before they actually have sexual intercourse. The time for the actual sex act may vary from a few minutes to much longer. Sometimes a couple may wish to take a lot of time making love, other times not. It is a matter of what each couple prefers.

Do adults always have orgasms when they have sex together?

Not always. Making love together is a learning process that can take a lot of time and experience. Many couples need to learn what makes their bodies respond to each other. Usually, enough time and experience will give them good physical rapport.

Does having sexual intercourse feel good even if no one has an orgasm?

Usually. The feelings between two people having intercourse are usually warm and affectionate even when one partner does not have an orgasm. The fact that one partner is receiving pleasure from the sex act will make the other feel good.

If a woman doesn't have orgasms at first, can she learn to have them?

Most emphatically yes. Many, if not most, women do not experience orgasm at first. As anxiety about sexual intercourse lessens and there is more experience, women feel free to explore their sexual responsiveness. Masturbation helps one to learn about one's own particular way of becoming aroused and reaching orgasm. It will also help if during sexual intercourse a woman receives adequate stimulation to the clitoral area. For the majority of women it is the clitoris, not the vagina, that is the most sexually responsive organ. Due to lack of knowledge or inexperience on the part of both the man and the woman, the clitoral area is sometimes not adequately stimulated, and the woman has difficulty reaching orgasm. The movement of the penis within the vagina is sometimes not enough to stimulate the clitoris to orgasm, and different positions may be used which will allow for extra stimulation.

How can I tell if I'll enjoy sex when I grow up?

Just assume you will. Because there are still experiences and feelings that you are unable to feel now, it does not mean that you will never feel them. Do not worry. Most people gradually learn how to enjoy and feel comfortable with the sexual part of their personality. Eventually they form a loving relationship with another person and learn more about enjoying sex.

Does it mean I'm not normal if the idea of having sexual intercourse seems revolting?

Not at all. Sexual intercourse is far enough away from your present stage of development and place in life to sound this way to you. Many times youngsters think it absolutely disgusting that adults actually kiss each other on the mouth. And of course, when they grow up, it no longer seems that way to them at all. They end up doing and liking some of the very same things that once seemed so terrible! As you grow older and develop different kinds of feelings toward yourself and toward the opposite sex, your feelings about sex will gradually change.

What do you do if you grow up and discover you just don't like having sex?

First of all, you will not grow up and suddenly discover this. You have lots of time, all during your growing up, to get used to sexual feelings and sexual thoughts. Gradually these will grow and develop and continue doing so into your adulthood. Any problems about "not liking sex" can usually be worked out with the right person, under the right kind of conditions. It is sometimes hard to imagine liking feelings or sensations with which you have had no experience.

Do old people have sexual intercourse?

Adults of all ages can and do enjoy sexual activity. Parents included. Grandparents included. In later years, the capacity for sexual arousal diminishes, and the frequency of sexual intercourse diminishes. If their health is good, many older people continue to enjoy the sexual part of their lives.

Would sexual intercourse feel different to a teen-ager than it would to an adult?

Any difference in feeling would be due to the fact that teenagers have had less time and experience in feeling comfortable with each other physically—or emotionally. Adolescents often feel very unsure of themselves, and this can interfere with enjoyment during sexual intercourse. No matter what the age, first experiences with sex involve a lot of learning, and they can be disappointing for some. It takes time to learn how to love someone—even physically.

How often do people have sexual intercourse with each other?

Frequency of sexual intercourse is a very personal and individual matter and can vary considerably. Usually young adults have sexual intercourse more frequently than older adults. Surveys show that young adults average sexual intercourse several times a week, and older adults less often.

Do adults ever have sex with someone they don't love?

Some do. Adults, just like adolescents, are learning about a lot of different feelings, sexual ones too. Most adults find sex more fulfilling when shared with someone they love.

CHAPTER FOUR

Pregnancy

CONCEPTION

It is an amazing phenomenon that one microscopic sperm out of millions of other sperm, destined to survive only a few hours, can find one tiny egg. Yet meet they do, and a new life is conceived in that instant.

During a female's monthly menstrual cycle, she is able to become pregnant for only a very short time—perhaps a few days. The exact time of fertility is difficult to pinpoint, but it is generally around the midway point between menstrual periods. For example, in a twenty-eight-day menstrual cycle, the most fertile period is from the tenth to the eighteenth day. In a thirty-day cycle the most fertile time would occur anywhere from the twelfth to the twentieth day. If a female has intercourse either too long before or too long after an egg has been released from an ovary, she will not become pregnant.

During the fertile period in the menstrual cycle, an egg, called an ovum, is released from one of the ovaries and begins its journey through the fallopian tubes and down into the uterus. If a couple have sexual intercourse during this fertile time without using any birth control, the male's sperm will travel up the vagina, through the cervix, swim into the uterus, and perhaps meet and fertilize the egg somewhere along this monthly route.

The sperm are microscopic in size, and there are hundreds of millions of them. They have tails that whip back and forth and

F\ EMALE E\ GG

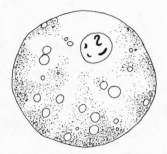

propel them upward through the uterus. This lasts only a short time, for in a day or two they lose their power to fertilize the female egg and die. That is why no pregnancy occurs unless the sperm meets the egg in this period of time.

When a sperm meets an egg, it immediately penetrates the outer covering of the egg, and conception takes place at that moment. No other sperm can then penetrate the egg. No one can know which sperm it will be. But which sperm it is determines whether a girl or a boy is to be born. The male sperm carries the determining sex factor. It has either an X chromosome or a Y chromosome. The eggs always carry an X chromosome. If a sperm carrying an X chromosome combines with an egg, there will be two X chromosomes, and the baby will be a female. If it happens that a sperm with a Y chromosome combines with an egg, there will be a combination of X and Y chromosomes, and the baby will be a male.

A fertilized egg will attach itself to a place within the wall of the uterus. The lining of tissue and blood, which is prepared within the uterus each month whether or not an egg is fertilized, will now come into use. The fertilized egg will develop in the uterus for the next nine months and change from an invisible speck into a fully developed baby.

Egg and Sperm Meeting in Fertilization

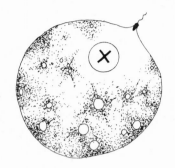

FEMALE COMBINATION XX   MALE COMBINATION XY

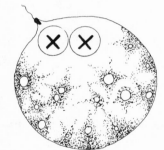   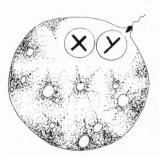

Fertilized Eggs Showing Sex Chromosomes

How does the egg know when it gets fertilized?

The egg doesn't *know* anything. When the egg becomes fertilized, it automatically begins to develop into a baby. It is genetically coded to respond to fertilization.

How does the egg choose where to attach itself in the uterus?

It just does. It may be chance, or position, or warmth that guides it. But it usually picks out a very good spot.

Can you get pregnant any other way than by sexual intercourse?

No. You cannot get pregnant if you touch sperm or kiss or anything of that sort.

If a man ejaculates near a woman's vagina, can the sperm make its way up her vagina and get her pregnant?

If the seminal fluid is very near the entrance to the vagina, it is possible (although unlikely) that the sperm could swim up the vagina in the vaginal secretions present. If the seminal fluid were in the vicinity, on a thigh or the pubic hair, it would be impossible for the sperm to enter the vagina.

Can you get pregnant with another baby if you are already pregnant?

No. While a woman is pregnant, she cannot get pregnant again until the child is born and her ovaries once again begin producing eggs.

Does a man always have sperm?

Usually yes. Unless an unusual medical condition exists where the man produces no sperm, there is always sperm in the seminal fluid, the liquid that carries the sperm. Even though you may not be able to "see" the sperm, you can safely assume that they are there.

Can a woman get pregnant if she doesn't have an orgasm during sex?

Yes. Once the woman's egg has been released it is available to become fertilized no matter what the woman experiences sexually. Only men have to have an orgasm in order to be able to ejaculate sperm in the seminal fluid.

Can a woman tell right away if she's gotten pregnant?

No. There is no physical sensation of "being fertilized." The only way a woman may suspect she is pregnant is if she misses a monthly menstrual period. This is usually the first sign. There are no menstrual periods during the entire pregnancy. And yet, a woman may miss menstrual periods and not be pregnant. The only way to make sure is to visit a doctor. Special tests can verify if she really is pregnant.

Is the egg alive?

The egg is alive just as the sperm is. Each contains life-giving elements, but each will die unless it meets and unites with the other.

How does the egg move from the ovary to the uterus?

Thousands of tiny hairlike tufts line the fallopian tubes and are constantly in motion, propelling the egg along. You cannot feel the movement of an egg.

Does more than one egg ever come out of an ovary?

Usually not. But if two eggs are released *at the same time*, they both might become fertilized, and a woman could have *nonidentical* twins. *Identical* twins occur when one fertilized egg splits in half and each half develops into a separate baby. Since they come from the same egg-sperm combination, the two babies look exactly alike.

Can you tell if the baby will be a boy or a girl?

Not really. Unless the mother has special tests for other medical reasons and asks to be told the sex, she will not know until the birth of her baby. Someday it may be possible for parents to choose the sex of their baby-to-be.

Is it dangerous to have a baby when you are a teen-ager?

It is not a good idea, physically or emotionally, to have children before you are fully grown and developed, which is usually after the age of seventeen or eighteen. Even though your body may be ready for it early, having and nursing a child is a great responsibility. It is best to wait until you can comfortably assume all the emotional responsibilities of being a mother or father, because it changes your way of life for many years to come.

DEVELOPMENT

The fertilized egg attaches itself to a spot in the uterus by means of a tiny cord and instantly begins to divide—and divide—and divide again. The divisions result in millions of cells that make up the different parts of your body.

The place in the uterus where the egg attaches itself develops into a special organ called a placenta. The tiny cord that attaches the developing baby to the placenta grows and acts as a channel for the nourishment the mother's body provides. The oxygen and nutrients in the mother's blood go through the placenta and on through the cord directly to the developing baby. The cord forms in what eventually will be the middle of the baby's stomach. It is called an umbilical cord. After birth this cord will be cut and will leave the only telltale physical mark of the baby's life inside its mother, the belly button.

By ten weeks the fetus is already so complex a creature that eyelids have formed and closed. By twelve weeks a human shape is apparent, the head, arms, fingers, legs, body, and face have all begun to develop. The male or female sex is apparent. At sixteen weeks the beating of the tiny heart can be heard with an obstetrical stethoscope, and the muscular movements of the rapidly growing fetus may be felt by the pregnant mother as fluttering bumps inside her lower abdomen. Every single thing down to the last eyelash and fingernail will be developed well before the baby is born. At birth it will weigh approximately six or seven pounds and be approximately 18 or 19 inches long.

The last one or two months of pregnancy the baby spends growing and fattening up inside the uterus. It kicks, turns, squirms, stretches, sucks its thumb, and probably dreams. It may also cry. It will be completely helpless, but now, at the end of forty weeks, it is ready to be born.

DEVELOPMENT OF THE HUMAN EMBRYO

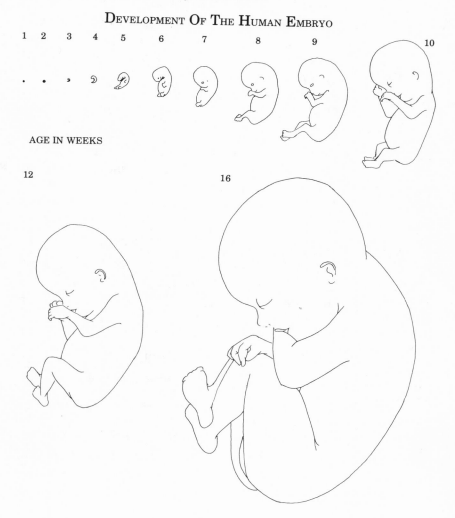

How does a baby breathe inside the mother?

A baby does not need to breathe for itself until it is born. During pregnancy the mother's lungs work for both her and the baby, giving her blood oxygen that is passed on to the baby's bloodstream by the placenta. When the baby is born, it must take in oxygen as we do, through its own mouth and lungs.

Does the baby eat while it is developing?

No. The baby's nourishment comes from the mother's blood. It is transmitted through the placenta to the umbilical cord, which passes it directly into the baby's bloodstream. No food goes through its mouth until after it is born, but it receives all the food, vitamins, and minerals it needs.

Does the baby have bowel movements?

Babies do not have bowel movements until after they are born. They do however produce urine. Their waste product is eventually excreted by the mother.

Are the eyes open?

A developing baby's eyes are open until eyelids form, at the end of the ninth week. Then the eyes are closed. There is some evidence that the baby can perceive light even while in the uterus. When the baby is born and the eyes open, the baby can "see," but the baby does not know what he or she is looking at.

Can the mother hear the baby move around or cry?

No. It is impossible to hear a cry. You can feel movements, but not hear them.

When the baby kicks and moves, does it hurt the mother?

No. The movements of the baby are cushioned by the sac of

water surrounding it as well as by the layers of muscle in the uterus. Even though the kicks may be strong, the parts of the mother's body the baby kicks at are flexible, so it does not hurt. Most mothers are happy to feel the kick because it lets them know their baby is alive and growing. Mothers may worry if they do not feel any movement. Fathers and sometimes brothers and sisters like to put their hands on the mother's stomach to feel the baby when it moves.

Does a baby feel anything inside the uterus or when it is being born?

The baby can feel warmth and cold, bumps and movement when it is inside the uterus. It is probably very used to the noise of the mother's heartbeat and rhythm. While it is being born, it may feel the sensations of being pushed and squeezed about a bit, but it does not know as we do that it is in the process of "being born." After birth the baby reacts very strongly to all kinds of stimuli, such as lights and sounds in the world around it.

CHAPTER FIVE

Birth

During the time the fetus is developing, the uterus painlessly and progressively stretches to fit the needs of the bigger and bigger baby. At the beginning the uterus is the size of a small closed fist. At the end it is the size of a watermelon.

The expandable house the baby has lived in for forty weeks now expands no longer. Hormones, size, and other body messages trigger the uterus to grow rigid and attempt to push the baby out by powerful muscle contractions. These are called labor pains, and they will expel the baby from the uterus into the world outside.

The massive muscles now contract regularly, stretching open the mouth of the uterus, called the cervix, until it is wide enough for the baby to pass through. The strong uterine muscles continue to work, pushing the baby down through this opening and into the vagina. The vagina now becomes the "birth canal" to the outside world. It expands to allow the baby through. The elastic opening of the vagina is also stretched open to allow the baby to come out.

Once the head of the baby is through this vaginal opening, the rest of its body quickly slips through, and the child is born. The umbilical cord is attached to the baby's stomach and trails the placenta behind it (the organ that supplied nourishment to the developing embryo). The cord is tied and cut, and a new child cries out.

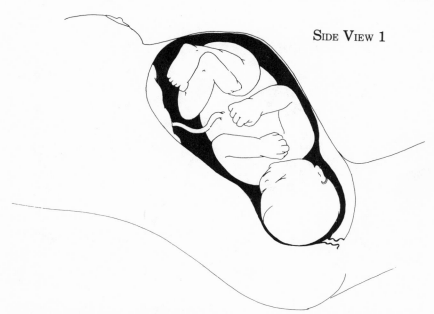

SIDE VIEW 1

LABOR CONTRACTIONS BEGIN TO PUSH THE BABY THROUGH THE BIRTH CANAL

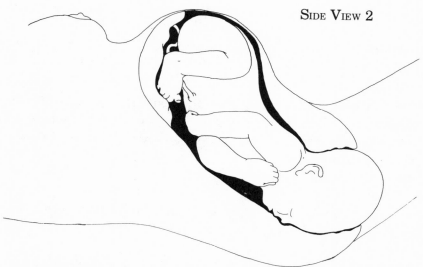

SIDE VIEW 2

LABOR CONTRACTIONS CONTINUE AND THE BABY'S HEAD BEGINS TO EMERGE FROM THE OPENING OF THE BIRTH CANAL

SIDE VIEW 3

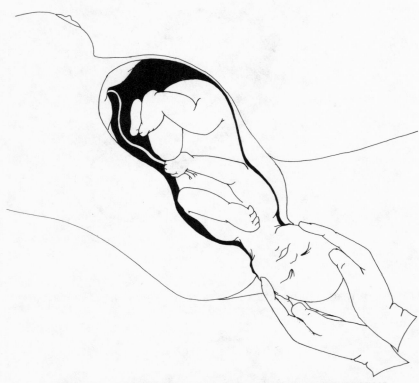

LABOR CONTRACTIONS PUSH THE BABY'S HEAD OUT OF THE VAGINAL
OPENING AND THE REST OF THE BODY QUICKLY FOLLOWS

The work of the uterus is now done, and it begins to contract quickly down to its original size. In a few weeks it will have returned to its normal size of a closed fist and its functions of monthly menstrual cycles.

I just can't believe I would ever be able to have a baby. Does anyone else feel that way?

Yes. Some adult men and women feel that way. They are utterly amazed when they indeed combine to produce something as wonderful as another human being. Sometimes it is very hard for any girl or woman to believe that she really has the capacity to produce and give birth to a normal healthy baby with the right number of toes and fingers. Until she sees it, she may not believe she is able to do such a phenomenal thing.

How does something as big as a baby come out of a place as small as the vagina?

The elastic nature of the vaginal walls allows for the passage of the baby. Even the outer opening to the vagina is stretchable enough to allow a baby to come through. The doctor usually helps a little here. He opens this portion of the vagina even further with a small incision called an episiotomy. This allows the baby's body to slip out quite easily. After birth this is repaired with a few stitches and soon heals.

Does it hurt when a baby is born?

It does hurt a lot, but it is the most easily bearable pain in the world because the result is so wonderful. Besides, there are many ways a doctor can ease the pain, either with anesthesia or by making sure that the woman has been well prepared by participation in natural-childbirth classes.

What does natural childbirth *mean?*

It means giving birth as naturally as possible, with the least amount of medication being given. Many pregnant women and their husbands attend natural childbirth classes and are instructed in the process of birth. In these classes the woman learns how to breathe at certain times during the birth process and how to posture her body in order to help the labor pains do their work. The aim of these classes is to allow the parents-to-be to assist in the birth by being relaxed, informed, and not tense. Mothers are able to tolerate labor much easier with this instruction and can deliver their babies with less need for anesthesia. Both mother and father can share and savor, with full awareness and joy, this most significant moment in their lives together.

Does the mother bleed when a baby is born?

There is no bleeding while the labor pains are in progress. After the baby is out of the vaginal opening and the placenta comes out of the uterus, there is some bleeding. This kind of bleeding is like a heavy menstrual period and will continue for a few days longer.

Can you die during childbirth?

The female body is built for delivering babies and even if no one were around to help, the mother could have a baby and not die. However, every so often a mother does die during childbirth. This is very, very unusual, and is usually caused by a serious medical condition that made her ill before the pregnancy. Most women do not have to worry about dying if they are regularly taken care of by an obstetrician.

Are you awake when the baby is being born?

Usually yes. The doctor may use some anesthetic toward the end of the delivery, but this does not put the mother to sleep. Most mothers are so excited about seeing their baby that they want to be awake every second of this happy time and not miss anything! Anesthesia that puts mothers to sleep also makes labor pains more sluggish, so doctors use special kinds that ease the pain and keep mothers awake too. Good strong labor and an awake mother help the baby to be born more easily and in better health.

What will happen if you aren't in a hospital and the baby starts to be born?

Usually, no matter where you are, there will be enough people around to help. Fathers can help while a baby is being born, so can taxi drivers, policemen, almost anyone—even the mother can help. Babies are born every day with no help from anyone at all.

Can you tell when the baby is about to be born?

Yes. First a mother feels the labor pains start, in the lower back and abdomen. These are usually weak and about half an hour apart. Later on, the labor contractions come closer together and are much stronger. Usually at some point during the labor process there will be a rush of water from the vagina. This means that the "bag of waters," which surrounded and cushioned the baby, has now broken. The water bag breaks in order to make it easier for the baby to slide through the birth canal and be born. Finally, the mother will feel the urge to begin pushing, as if in a very strong bowel movement. This is such a strong physical urge, it is almost impossible to resist. At this point in labor the mother knows the baby will be born very soon.

How long does it take for a baby to be born?

Counting all the hours of labor, a first baby usually takes about twelve hours to be born. Later babies take less time. The longest part of labor is the early contractions of the first stage, when the uterine muscles begin to stretch open the cervix in order for the baby to be pushed out into the birth canal. The last stage of labor, when the baby is actually being pushed out of the uterus through the vagina, goes much faster.

What are fathers supposed to do while their babies are being born?

Some fathers like to sit outside the delivery room and wait for the good news. Other fathers like to share every minute, right from the start, including all the labor and delivery! There are many birth-training classes for mothers and fathers together where parents-to-be learn all about labor and birth together.

During labor, fathers can time the contractions and remind their wives when to relax and when to help push down. Just their presence gives their wives a tremendous amount of emotional support. Watching the birth, they can share the experience and are not left outside as if it were not their baby too! More and more fathers now have a place in the delivery room, not just the waiting room.

Where inside the hospital is the baby born?

During labor the mother is usually in a special "labor room." There she can relax and wait with her husband for the actual birth time. Nurses check her, and the doctor visits her. When it is almost time for the baby to be born, she is moved into a "delivery room." This is a hospital operating room. It is very, very clean and has all the kinds of equipment necessary to help ensure a healthy, safe birth for both mother and baby. Afterward, she is taken to a regular hospital room to recover and get to know her new baby!

Do babies die during childbirth?

This very rarely happens, but sometimes it does. Every effort is made with modern medical techniques to save the life of a baby who is born ill or has little chance to survive, but sometimes these efforts cannot help. This is a terribly sad situation for the parents, but fortunately after a while they can try again.

What if a baby is too big to get out. Does the baby ever get stuck?

Babies are not too big to get out. If the baby is very big and the mother is very small, the doctor will be able to decide if she can deliver the baby the usual way or if he must perform a special operation called a Caesarian section. This is used if the mother cannot deliver the child through the vagina. Using anesthesia, which puts the mother to sleep, the doctor makes an incision through the lower abdomen and into the uterus, from which the doctor removes the baby. Then the incision is stitched closed, and the operation is over. Because doctors know ahead of time if the babies are able to be born in the usual manner or if a Caesarian birth is necessary, babies do not get stuck.

Does the baby ever come too early?

Sometimes. If a baby is born very, very early, before it is twenty-eight weeks old and under one pound in weight, it will have no chance of living. When the baby is not born alive at a very early stage, the mother is said to have had a miscarriage. Other times the baby may be born early, but further along in development than twenty-eight weeks and over two pounds. These babies have a slim chance and are called premature babies. Every effort is made to preserve such a baby's life by placing it in a hospital incubator where the baby receives warmth, rest, nutrients, and rich oxygen to breathe. Quite often these premature babies of only a few pounds are able to survive and grow up to lead entirely normal lives.

Are babies ever born too late?

Very rarely. If there is some problem with the timing of the birth, there are special techniques the doctor can use to bring about labor and delivery.

How do twins develop?

Twins develop in one of two ways. One way is from an egg which separates into two equal, identical parts, and each part develops into a baby. These babies are always of the same sex and look exactly alike. They are called identical twins.

The other way is when two eggs develop instead of one. If both eggs are fertilized by two different sperm, two different babies will develop. These babies are twins, but since they develop from two separate eggs and two separate sperm, they may not look alike, or be of the same sex.

If you have twins, how do they come out?

Twins are born one after the other, usually a few minutes apart. This normally is not a problem for the mother at all. In the case of Siamese twins—a very rare situation where the twins are attached physically to each other—doctors can use special operations to help the babies be born.

Are all babies born the same way?

No. The vast majority of babies are born head first. A few are born feet first. These are called breech babies. Either way, these are both delivered through the vagina.

Once the baby is born, is the mother's body the same as it was before?

The vagina returns to its original size, and in a few weeks the uterus is right back to where it was before. Right after the delivery the stomach gets pretty flat again. Mothers can usually get up and walk around the same day. The mother's body looks and feels the same, except that her breasts fill up with milk. Usually both mother and baby can go home after about three days.

How do I know whether to nurse my baby or give it a bottle?

Breast feeding provides both the mother and baby with special advantages. Babies thrive on mother's milk, and breast feeding provides an opportunity for a special closeness between mother and baby. If you do not feel comfortable breast feeding your baby, make sure that whenever you bottle-feed, your baby is held close in your arms.

Will my breasts get bigger and stretched during pregnancy and stay that way?

Breasts do enlarge under the influence of hormones during pregnancy and due to milk production, but this is a temporary state. Unless a lot of weight is gained, breasts should not stretch any substantial amount. Pregnancy does not permanently alter the size or shape of breasts.

What happens to the milk if the mother doesn't nurse the baby?

The doctor will administer medication that stops the milk production. In a few days the fullness of the breasts are reduced, and they have returned to their normal size and state.

Do all parents love their baby right away?

No. Most people who do love their baby immediately loved the idea of their baby very much. Usually babies are loved more than enough, and as time passes, even deeper parental love develops.

Does the baby know who its mother is right away?

A baby has to learn who its mother is. To babies, the person who always takes care of them, soothes them, feeds them, cuddles them, and loves them will be their mother, even if that person happens to be their father or a nurse. Mothering is a process, not just a physical birthright.

Is it normal to not want to have a baby?

Absolutely. All kinds of wants, likes, and dislikes change as people and situations in life change. If you do not want to have a baby now, you may grow up and still not want to have a baby. But it is just as possible that you may grow up, fall in love with someone, and decide that you want to share the experience of having a child with that person. You may end up wanting lots of babies. You may even decide you want a child but would rather adopt one than have one of your own! All are purely personal choices, not "normal" or "abnormal" ones.

What does a baby look like when it is born?

The baby is covered with a film of white cheeselike material, which has protected its skin while in the uterus. This is washed off. Its eyes are closed tight, and usually it is quite red from the exertion of crying and breathing all at once—and all for the first time. Sometimes it has quite a bit of hair, and sometimes it appears bald. It looks beautiful to all mothers and fathers!

CHAPTER SIX

Caution and
Precaution

BIRTH CONTROL

Along with adult love and sexual relationships comes a new kind of responsibility—the responsibility of protecting yourself and the one you care for from an unwanted pregnancy. Adults use birth control methods so that the birth of their children will come when they can be loved and cared for.

Most birth control methods simply stop the sperm from fertilizing the egg. This allows sexual intercourse without the fear of producing an unwanted pregnancy. When two people who love each other decide they want a child, they can decide to stop using birth control. Until then, it is necessary to be informed about how to prevent a pregnancy and to discuss with your partner the method of control you both wish to use.

There are many choices of birth control methods, although some are less effective than others. It is best to use the most reliable methods. When both people share the responsibility by each using a birth control device, they also double their security.

Here is a list of the types of practical birth control methods and how they are used:

- The condom, commonly called a rubber, is a very thin rubber sheath that slips over the penis. Sperm is collected in the space left at the tip. This sheath is taken off and thrown away after intercourse.

- The diaphragm is a thin rubber disc that is fitted by a physician, who will instruct the woman in its use. It is inserted into the vagina and covers the cervix so that sperm cannot enter. It is removed several hours after sexual intercourse, cleaned, and reused as necessary.

- Birth control pills must be prescribed by a physician. The hormones in these pills act upon the menstrual cycle to prevent pregnancy.

- The IUD is an intrauterine device. It is a small coil or loop of plastic or copper that a physician inserts into the uterus. Somehow it interferes with conception.

- Spermicidal foam, cream, or jelly may be inserted directly into the vagina with a special applicator and should be applied directly before sexual intercourse. They are used in conjunction with other birth control devices such as a condom or diaphragm because alone they are not a very effective method of birth control.

What is the best birth control method to use?

The best birth control method to use is any one that you will be sure to use always! The pill will not do anyone any good if even one or two days are missed. A condom put on carelessly will not do anyone any good. A diaphragm lying in someone's closet instead of being used to cover the cervix is useless too! There is no "best" birth control method—only a best method for each particular person and his or her needs. Birth control methods should be worked out carefully, and especially for a woman with her doctor's help.

Is a rubber unsafe in any way?

Yes. Since it is very fragile and easily punctured, as well as being liable to slip off easily, it must be used with great care. Space must always be left at the tip for the seminal fluid to collect, or the fluid will flow up over the top of the condom. It is best to use it in conjunction with a spermicidal foam or jelly.

Does it hurt to wear a rubber?

No. It is very thin and elastic and does not hurt or constrict the penis in any way.

Is a douche something that helps prevent pregnancy?

No. Douching after sexual intercourse does nothing to prevent pregnancy, no matter what you may have heard. Douches, consisting of a water bag and applicator, insert water into the vagina. This is supposed to wash the vaginal walls. It will certainly not wash away all the sperm in the seminal fluid. Using a douche may seem a lot easier than going to a doctor or buying reliable birth control aids, but it is also completely useless.

Is there anything besides a rubber a man can use? It seems unfair that women have to do so much.

Unfortunately, there is no birth control method like the pill available for men as yet. They can only use a condom. However, there is a permanent type of birth control operation called a vasectomy. Perhaps someday soon there will be an alternative birth control method that men can use.

Is the pill dangerous to use?

There is debate about this. Side effects and complications from long-term use of the pill are now beginning to appear more clearly. Physicians do not like to recommend the pill to women who have certain kinds of medical conditions or to women who only very occasionally have sexual relations. While the protection of the pill is virtually certain, a complete medical examination and very careful consideration with your doctor is advisable before deciding to use the pill.

Does being on the pill make you look or feel any different?

No one could tell you were on the pill by looking at you. But the pill does stimulate your hormones, and some women have various side effects. There can be a slight enlargement of the breasts or some weight gain due to water retention in the tissues. You may not feel any different physically, but the emotional effect of being on the pill may make you feel very different. Being on the pill is evidence of a sexual relationship, and this always has a wide range of emotional overtones.

Is it true that if you miss one day on the pill, you can get pregnant?

Yes. The hormone cycle the pill method stimulates must be very carefully followed. Your monthly menstrual period will occur during the few days of the month when you are off the pill. Any irregularity in taking the pill on the prescribed days can destroy its birth control effect.

What does a diaphragm feel like?

When a diaphragm is properly fitted and properly inserted, it cannot be felt by a woman at all. A woman knows it is there but not because of physical discomfort. In fact, many women tend to forget that it is in place.

My sister says that using a diaphragm makes sex too planned and mechanical. Is she right?

Only half right. It does mean that something was planned, but that does not make it mechanical. Sexual intercourse does not really happen out of the blue and usually is something that is planned, even if the people involved would rather think it was spontaneous. It is always better to be careful.

How many times can a woman have sexual intercourse without getting pregnant?

None. It may take only once if no birth control methods are used.

Should you obtain some birth control device —just in case?

"Just in case" means that someone is thinking about having sexual relations. It is a better idea to have a relationship that permits talking about it with your partner first, instead of letting something happen by accident.

What do you do if you are too embarrassed to talk about birth control precautions but are thinking about having sexual relations with someone?

You either go ahead and talk about it even though you are embarrassed, or you do not have any sexual relations until you can be open with your partner and are able to discuss it. In anything as intimate and personal as a sexual relationship, it is very important to feel free to talk about such important decisions. It will be better for you both and your relationship.

Are teen-agers allowed to buy condoms and other kinds of birth control aids?

There is no age prohibition upon birth control devices such as condoms and spermicidal foams and jellies. Diaphragms, pills, and IUDs are only prescribed by doctors or special birth control clinics, and most states place no prohibition of age upon their use.

Where can you buy condoms and spermicidal foams?

These are available in drugstores. Usually there is a display case near the pharmacy section with an assortment of condoms. If you do not see any, you will have to ask for them. Although this might be embarrassing, drugstores are so used to selling them that they take very little notice.

Will a doctor fit a teen-ager with a diaphragm or prescribe birth control pills for her?

Almost always yes. A doctor usually cares most about protecting the patient. He or she will make every effort to prescribe the best contraceptive geared to the girl's personal needs. Most doctors are pleased when a girl is responsible enough to protect herself intelligently.

If a girl goes to a doctor for birth control pills, will the doctor tell her parents?

No. Most doctors respect the privacy of their patients. The doctor could be specifically asked to withhold such personal information. Usually a doctor will respect this request. If the doctor will not, the girl can go elsewhere. There are many birth control clinics and Planned Parenthood chapters ready to help those who need it. And there are many parents, when given the chance, who would help obtain this kind of information and help.

Where can you find a doctor for birth control if you don't want to use your family doctor?

Usually a family doctor is the best person, one who knows you and will want to help you. But you can always call a large hospital or the local county medical society in your city and ask for a referral to an obstetrician-gynecologist or a birth control clinic.

Couldn't a couple just be very careful not to have sex when the female is in her fertile time?

No. This is an age-old method called the rhythm method. The only trouble with it is it does not work. Usually it is only used by couples who have very strict religious beliefs that prohibit the use of any birth control devices. The problem with this method is that it is too difficult to know exactly when the fertile time is. Anyone whose religious beliefs prohibit the use of a birth control device should really not be involved in a sexual relationship until he or she can love and support the children that might result from mistakes in timing. Using this method when one is not bound by religious beliefs is an excuse for avoiding a responsible and active role in one's own sex life. It may just seem easier and may allow a person to kid himself or herself about not being really involved in a sexual relationship. Anyone who has such feelings is not ready for a sexual relationship at all.

ABORTION

Abortion is the process whereby a medical doctor ends a very early pregnancy so it will not continue and develop into a full-term baby. This is usually done in a hospital by a doctor, using special instruments that empty the uterus. After the abortion the woman's menstrual cycle will resume, and she will no longer be pregnant.

People obtain abortions if they have become pregnant by mistake and definitely cannot care for and raise a child. Abortions are performed other times when the woman's health is in jeopardy or there is some question as to the health of the unborn baby.

Abortion is a loaded issue that many people, including physicians, disagree about. Those against abortion feel that it is the same as taking a life. Their own moral or religious beliefs dictate that every pregnant woman should allow her pregnancy to continue so that the baby can develop and live, unless some medical emergency requires aborting the pregnancy.

At least as many other people, who are for abortion, feel it should be made available to any woman who wants or needs it. They feel that without abortions disastrous situations are allowed to develop where an unwanted child will be forced upon one or both parents who are unable or unwilling to love and care for it, and all will suffer. They also believe that since the woman usually bears the brunt of both the physical and emotional burden of pregnancy, it should be up to her to decide if she is willing to continue a pregnancy. Their view is that abortion is not taking a life but is preventing life where it will cause much unhappiness and pain.

Those who believe abortion should be utilized do not feel it is another method of birth control, nor should it be used as such. It is only used where effective birth control methods fail. Any surgical procedure, no matter how simple it may seem, is best prevented in the interests of safety and health.

How far along in a pregnancy can you still get an abortion?

An abortion should be done as early as possible, preferably before the twelfth week. Once the egg has developed beyond twelve weeks, it is difficult to remove, and it can be a more dangerous process. Another, more complicated medical procedure has to be used, and it is always best to avoid that when possible. Of course, the further along in the pregnancy, the more difficult it becomes emotionally, too.

Are abortions dangerous?

Abortions can be very dangerous when not performed by a medically trained physician under special sanitary conditions such as hospitals provide. There have been tragic results from abortions obtained from untrained people performed under unsanitary conditions.

Does it hurt to have an abortion?

Abortions are done with an anesthetic that puts the woman to sleep (or removes most of the pain if she is awake). Without an anesthetic it would be painful. By the time the woman is fully awake, most of the physical pain is gone.

Does it hurt afterward?

Usually not. Aside from some mild cramps that might occur, most women have very few aftereffects. Some even return home the same day or the following day and are able to resume their activities feeling physically fine.

Do women feel bad afterward?

Most women feel a bitter-sweet blend of sadness or regret and relief—sadness because pregnancy is an event they wish they could have celebrated with joy and relief because it sets them free from the predicament the pregnancy posed. Few women are completely overjoyed.

How does the doctor end a pregnancy?

He or she opens the cervix enough to insert an instrument to remove its contents. When it is very early in a pregnancy, the egg is not yet very firmly attached to the uterus and comes out quite easily.

Does the baby feel the abortion?

The baby is at such a primitive stage of development that there is no ability to feel pain as we know it.

Can you still have more babies if you have an abortion?

Yes. You can have as many babies as you want to after an abortion.

Will a doctor perform an abortion on a teen-ager if her parents don't know about it?

Obtaining abortions if you are under eighteen is somewhat

more difficult when you do not have your parents' consent. While many doctors would perform such abortions, there may be state laws that prohibit medical treatment for minors without parental consent. Hospitals are bound by these state laws. While it may be possible to obtain an abortion outside of a hospital without the knowledge of parents, it is probably much safer to have them know and get the best medical care available.

Where can you get information about safe abortion clinics that do not require the consent of parents?

Most doctors can tell you what is available in your city. A local birth control clinic or a Planned Parenthood chapter will give advice and help. It is an emotionally heavy burden to bear as well as an important decision. Having parental support can be very helpful. Unlike in the darker days of the Victorian era, many parents will give this support gladly.

VENEREAL DISEASE

Venereal disease—commonly called VD—is a highly contagious disease involving male and female genitals and reproductive organs. Venereal disease can only be transmitted by having sexual intercourse with a person who has the disease. The germs, which cannot live for very long in air, can only be transmitted when the warm, wet part of one person touches the warm, wet part of another person. Usually this involves genital-to-genital contact. Rarely can VD be caught from any source except this kind of direct sexual contact.

Venereal disease can be cured easily, but it is important to treat it early. It is very important to consult a doctor if you notice any unusual symptoms associated with your sexual organs. Venereal disease is much more common than most people imagine.

There are two common types:

- Gonorrhea, also known as the clap, is dangerous because it can be a silent disease. You can have it and not know that you do. It is highly contagious. In males, it usually shows itself by pain in the penis and by a discharge from the penis. In females, there may be a discharge from the vagina, or there may just be some pain when a pelvic inflammatory condition develops. But most of the time in females there are no symptoms at all, or they may be so slight as to escape notice. It is very important therefore to visit a doctor for regular gynecologic check-ups when you are having a sexual relationship. These check-ups will greatly minimize the risk of not noticing the presence of gonorrhea.

- Syphilis usually starts out as a small ulcer on the penis, and in females, a small ulcer in the vagina. This disease progresses through stages that bring on more and more severe disorders.

Herpes Genitalis

Herpes genitalis is a virus which affects the male or female genitals. It is passed from one partner to another during sexual intercourse. Infection results in clusters of blisters which may become secondarily infected. It is important to have this condition treated promptly.

Is VD dangerous?

Only if untreated. Gonorrhea, for example, can cause sterility. Syphilis, if not treated, can cause death.

Can you catch VD just by dancing with or talking to someone who has it?

No. You can talk and dance without worrying.

Can you catch VD by kissing someone who has it?

This is so unlikely as to be almost impossible. VD germs live in the genitals and will infect only other genitals that touch them.

How can you know for sure if you have VD?

You can't, and that is why if you have any doubt, despite your embarrassment or fear or whatever, see a doctor.

Will a doctor tell your parents if you go for VD treatment?

No. Especially not if you ask him or her to keep the information confidential. The doctor may, however, be required by law to report any VD cases to the local health department. The health department is required to keep this information confidential and makes every effort not to let anyone know. If you are concerned about this, ask the doctor how you can protect your privacy. Don't let this stop you or anyone you know from seeing a doctor. A doctor will respect and respond to your wishes about confidential information.

Do you have to tell the doctor whom you had sexual contact with?

No, you don't have to, but it makes good sense to do so, and to tell your friend as well. A person may not realize he or she has VD and may spread the disease to others. This way the person can get proper treatment. It is not like "turning someone in"; rather, you will be helping him or her get cured.

Why does the health department want to know?

Because VD is such a highly contagious disease, the government feels responsible for protecting the welfare of others. They want to make sure that anyone who has it, as well as the ones they have come in contact with, get proper treatment and are cured.

What can I do to make sure I never catch VD?

In sexual relationships there is always the risk of VD, but this can be greatly minimized because there are many things you can do to help prevent VD. Soap and water are enemies of VD. Condoms offer a great deal of protection to both parties. You can be careful with whom you have a sexual relationship. (Statistics show VD is much more common among very sexually active people who have several sexual partners.) But most important, at the first sign of any trouble, see a doctor. You shouldn't live in fear of VD, but it is something to know about and not to ignore.

CHAPTER SEVEN

Feelings

FEELINGS ABOUT THE OPPOSITE SEX

Adolescence is a time of profound change. Not just changes in your body and how it feels, looks, and functions but in your emotional feelings. And one of the most noticeable changes in your feelings may be the way you feel toward members of the opposite sex.

Seemingly worlds apart, boys and girls experience puberty in much the same way. Adolescence for both offers the same hurdles, the same questions and self-doubts, and the same new prideful discoveries.

In adolescence you begin to have increased awareness about each other. You begin by daydreaming, fantasizing, and talking about members of the opposite sex. This is usually the first step before actual relationships take place.

At first you will probably be together in large groups, like school functions, parties, dances, or summer camp. After a while, your group will become a little smaller and more selective; perhaps it will be a club or a large group of friends from the same grade. You will meet each other in a more intense and intimate fashion and begin to notice details in personalities. These groups are important because they give you the chance to seek out people and to get close, without getting too close.

After a good deal of these experiences you will probably narrow down the group even further to a few close friends, some of the same sex and some of the opposite sex.

Small group activities, such as parties, trips, and so forth, will allow you to get close to one person for longer and longer times. Through these group activities you try out a wide variety of roles and contacts and slowly gain the experience that allows you to have closer relationships.

After being with the opposite sex in groups and feeling more comfortable with boy-girl relationships, you will eventually want to be with one special person. Dating is an exciting yet scary time. Usually this is true for everyone. There is always fear of unknown territory and untested ground.

In the beginning, especially on first dates, there are always inner qualms: What do you talk about? What do you do? What will he or she think of you? Will the person want to see you again? How do you let him or her know you'd like to be together again? All these worries have at their heart your fear of rejection.

Later on, as you begin to gain experience in single dating and being alone with someone, you may feel more at ease with the idea of "liking" someone in a new way. You may feel that you like him or her very much and begin to wonder, "Am I in love?" Love, once so far away may now seem very near.

Some people do not think about "being in love" with someone until much later on in adulthood. Some people have a wonderful time just liking, looking, thinking, and feeling but do not need to label the experience as being "in love" as yet. Others, however, may feel that the very intense liking they feel should be called love.

It can be very difficult to distinguish love from a lot of other emotions that may be felt toward someone of the opposite sex.

You may like the idea of being in love and think that these strange new feelings must be love. "Loving the way you look at me" and "loving the way you look" bring a lot of feelings that may make you feel that love has arrived! There is one thing that unites all these feelings. They are new; they are exciting; and they are happening to you!

As more time is spent alone with this person of the opposite sex exploring the new emotional relationship, some sexual exploring will take place also. Growing up can be one of the hardest things a person will ever do. This road is even harder if you learn about sexual feelings with people you find you cannot like, respect, or trust. It is good to have a friend in the boy or girl with whom you learn about this special part of growing up.

This brings us to the other side of these new feelings and relationships with the opposite sex, the lonely and painful parts. It can be lonely and painful when it seems that the whole world is separating into pairs of two, except you. You can feel miserably left out, but you will simply have to trust that your time will come later on.

It can be very difficult when you feel you like someone very much who does not feel the same way about you. Even if he or she does, you may fear that they will stop feeling that way or that you will. Often that is exactly what happens.

No matter how serious, important, and intense your love may feel, it will usually change as time goes by. You will change. Your friend will change, and what you thought would last forever may end.

All these feelings, good ones and bad ones, are all part of growing up.

When is it all right to go out on a date alone?

Usually by the time you want to go out on a date with one special person, you are arriving at the age when single dating is appropriate. Don't go out on a single date just because you want to do what everyone else is doing or because you want to do what no one else is doing. Wait until you have better reasons, more suited to your more individual feelings.

Is something wrong with you if you don't like dating?

Absolutely not. Many people do not start dating one single

person until late in adolescence or early adulthood. It is not unusual for girls and boys of the same age to have widely different feelings about dating. You may not like the idea of dating because you have not had enough time really to get to know people of the opposite sex and to feel comfortable with them. Give yourself this time.

Why does it seem that girls always run after boys?

Girls, who mature faster, may be ready for relationships with boys before boys get to the same stage. Usually when this is the case, girls do run after boys—but only until the boys are old enough to become interested in them!

Is it all right for a girl to ask a boy out?

Of course. There is no sense in playing games about who has the right to ask and who has to sit and wait. Girls should be able to ask boys out whenever they want to, and boys should be able to refuse whenever they want to! Each should really feel free to contact the other.

I want to go out on dates, but why am I scared?

You just have not had the experience. Not having that kind of experience behind you, you are assuming that you may be rejected or not know what to do or say. When you are ready and really want to date, you will try it even though you may still feel anxious. Time and experience will gradually lessen your anxiety.

If you go out on a date alone with someone, does that person expect you to kiss them?

Both of you are probably wondering the same thing. It is not expected, but it is thought about! Probably you will kiss if you both feel like it.

What makes me so nervous when I'm around someone of the opposite sex?

Fear. You are worried that the other person will think you are not good, smart, clever, witty, or gorgeous enough. You fear you won't be able to think of something charming, clever, or wonderful to say or that you just won't look right. In short, you are really worried about the other person not liking you.

Why do I care so much if someone likes me?

As you give up a very intimate relationship with parents, your friends fill the gap. Everyone needs to be liked, and during adolescence this need begins to be transferred from the need for parental approval to the need for approval from friends.

What does make out *mean?*

It means that a boy and girl kiss and perhaps sexually touch each other. It is making love without actually having sexual intercourse. Some people call it petting, others necking.

What does first base, second base, *and* third base *mean?*

First base refers to a boy and girl just kissing. *Second base* refers to any touching of the body above the waist, such as the breasts. *Third base* means touching each other below the waist. It is a shorthand way of talking about subjects without using the actual words.

What is a French kiss?

This is when one or both people want to touch tongues or explore the inside of their mouths with their tongues during a kiss.

Should you make out with someone if he or she is just a date and not someone with whom you are going steady?

"Shoulds" and "should nots" do not apply to everyone or to every situation. It is better to have less sexual activity with people you do not know very well or care about.

Is the boy supposed to make the first advance to the girl?

Boys usually make the first move. But usually not until the girl has given an unspoken message that such action would be welcome! Eyes, smiles, body movements, words—all combine to give these messages. A boy should be aware that a girl sometimes just wants to flirt and go no further.

What do you do if a boy expects a lot of sexual action and you don't want any?

You simply let him know how you feel. And you don't go out with anyone who won't respect the way you feel! Part of liking someone is finding out whether you like him or her despite the things you disagree about. You should not have to have sexual activity to keep a relationship together or to conform to what others do.

How old do you have to be before you start going together?

Going together, or going steady, is something people do when they want to be with each other and no one else. This is not so much dependent upon actual age as it is upon how much previous experience there has been in boy-girl relationships. Usually people have had previous experience dating a lot of different people before they want to start this kind of special arrangement. Going together for days, weeks, or months provides a nice close relationship with someone of the opposite sex, but it is also good to get to know different kinds of people.

If a girl and boy are going together, is it all right for them to make out with someone else?

This can make the other person feel very hurt, unless the

couple have agreed on it beforehand. Going together is like closing the door to other people so that the two of you can feel as if you belong very much to each other and to no one else. Making out with someone else is like opening the door and letting someone else into this private relationship. Perhaps the desire to make out with someone else signals that it really is time to stop going together and start dating a lot of other people.

Can you be a teen-ager and still be in love?

You can feel as though you are in love. Later on in life, looking back, you may realize that you were learning about your feelings. Love later on in life, or love that grows, usually is more complex than teen-age love. This does not mean it is more intense. Teen-age love can be very poignant and tender because it is so young and uncomplicated and does not carry with it the adult responsibility of marriage and children.

Can you love someone even if you only go together for a week?

You might feel that way. Later on, you may see it was not love.

Can you fall out of love in a day or two?

Probably not. If you care for, trust, and love someone, it is not so easy to stop in a day or two.

Why am I so jealous if someone I like goes out with someone else?

Jealousy rears its head way back in infancy. Babies are jealous if their mother is occupied with something else for too long. Children are jealous of their brothers and sisters, other children, someone else's toys, and so on and so forth. Grown-ups are jealous. Jealousy is something you just have to learn to recognize as a holdover from the days of wanting to be the only one—the only one loved, the only one with a toy, the only one with attention, and so forth.

What does going all the way *mean?*

It means going beyond making out and having sexual intercourse. There are all kinds of slang expressions for this. No matter what word is used, it does not mean the experience is bad or shameful.

Why do some boys act as though having sex with someone is something to be recorded, like a football score or a home run?

This is a relic from the days of the double standard, when girls were not supposed to have sexual feelings and boys were supposed to be sexual. To protect a "he-man" concept of themselves, a boy or man needed to consider making love a physical victory rather than a shared and intimate experience.

Are boys more turned on by sex than girls?

No. Sexual activity for boys has always been sanctioned, whereas sexual activity for girls has been frowned upon by society. "Good" girls were supposed to be less sexual. Nowadays, women do not need to hide their own sexuality, and girls should feel free to satisfy their sexual needs. Women do not usually talk about their relationships only as a sexual matter but rather in combination with emotions of love and trust. This may also lead to the mistaken notion that females are not as turned on by sex as males.

Why do some girls sexually tease boys?

Both boys and girls experiment with their new powers of sexual attraction. Some girls, trying to prove they are desirable, arouse more feelings than they are prepared to handle. Most girls are sensitive to the intensity of sexual feelings and try not to be deliberately provocative.

If a girl makes out with a boy, will he put her down for it when he is with his friends?

Probably not, but if he does, it is unlikely any girl would even want to go out with him! Any boy or man who resorts to "putting someone down" for this is only reflecting badly upon himself.

Should teen-agers experiment with sex?

At some point in life, whether it be during adolescence or later, some sexual experimentation is normal. It is important, however, that this be basically between two people who feel good about each other, are roughly at the same level of sexual experience, and are roughly in the same age group. When expectations, experiences, and feelings differ too widely, someone may be hurt. It is also important that both people take care that there are no bad consequences for either of them, such as feeling guilty, hurt, ashamed, or getting pregnant. It is fine to have sexual desires and feelings about the opposite sex without having to justify it by "being in love." At this stage in life, when you are learning about sexual and emotional feelings, having trust and respect for each other is important.

Is there a difference between love and sex?

It is sometimes difficult to tell the two apart. For some people there is a difference, and for others there is not. Usually, however, at least at first, there is a difference between love and sexual feelings. Sexual desire is a need for the physical part of the relationship, the act of making love. Love requires deeper caring and trusting and fills inner emotional needs. Relationships with the opposite sex can bring a variety of combinations of these feelings. Some relationships may be dominated by sexual feelings. In other relationships, the love emotions may be foremost. Eventually, relationships with the opposite sex usually contain a healthy blend of these two kinds of feelings. It is good to be aware that these emotions can exist somewhat independently, so you don't have to pretend that love exists where it does not.

When is it all right to go all the way?

This depends. Some people feel comfortable having a sexual relationship before marriage whether or not they are deeply in love. Others feel there must be a deep, serious love relationship present. Still others feel a need for the security and trust of a marriage relationship, and still others simply have religious or moral beliefs that do not allow sex before marriage. What is really important is for each person to know when he or she is in a position to enjoy having a sexual relationship before marriage. It should make both people feel good, not guilty, sad, or threatened in any way. It is a very special personal decision, based not just upon love but upon a lot of understanding between two people of themselves, each other, and their relationship.

Does anyone ever tell his or her friends or parents about their sexual experiences?

Usually not in great detail, if they tell at all. By the time you have close emotional and sexual relationships, you may not want to share these intimate experiences. But it is also possible that you may wish to talk about some of your feelings with a close friend or parent.

Does everyone have sexual intercourse at some time?

Most everyone. Usually people who are involved in a romantic way experience sexual intercourse. There are some people who are never involved in any kind of relationship with the opposite sex, and they may never have sexual intercourse, but this is rare. There are others who prefer relationships with only people of their own sex, and they may never experience sexual intercourse, although this too is rare.

What does homosexual *mean?*

Homosexual refers to a man who prefers to have love and sexual relationships with other men rather than with women.

When women want to have love and sexual relationships with other women, they are called lesbians. Being heterosexual is the more usual state of affairs, one in which men and women want sexual love and relationships with members of the opposite sex.

How can you tell if you will be a homosexual or a lesbian?

You usually cannot and really don't have to worry about it. Anxieties like these can be brought about by the wide and obvious differences between people of the same age. Some boys or girls your own age may be very sexually developed and have relationships with the other sex while you feel no inclination or ability to do the same. This can foster fears and questions regarding your own identity. This does not mean that you are not as masculine or feminine as the others. It only means that you are operating on different time schedules.

Is it normal to have fantasies about people of your own sex?

Yes. During adolescence feelings about yourself, the opposite sex, and the same sex, are all bubbling to the surface of your mind. It is normal to have some fantasies about the same sex. Most people do not act upon these thoughts. Others are so upset about such feelings that they quickly exclude all such thoughts from their conscious mind and deny they ever existed.

I like going out with girls, but I don't want to make out with them or have sex. Does that mean I might be a homosexual?

No. You are simply trying to find out about girls as people first. Later on, when you grow older, more sexual and romantic feelings will enter your relationships.

I don't like being around girls. Is that the way homosexuals feel?

No. In adolescence it is very normal for boys and girls not to like being with each other. It takes time to feel comfortable with people of the opposite sex. When there are no sisters or brothers in a family, it can take a longer time to get used to being in a group of the opposite sex. Later on, after you have more experience, you will feel very differently about being with girls. Homosexuals generally do not dislike girls; they simply are sexually attracted to other males and often would rather be female themselves.

Does the way you look have anything to do with being a homosexual or a lesbian?

No. Homosexuals can be huge, muscular "he-men" who look very masculine, and lesbians can be very beautiful and feminine-appearing women. Sexual preferences for the same sex are a psychological state, not a physical one. Many boys worry about not looking male enough. Girls worry if they look too masculine. Looks just do not matter. The way people feel about themselves does.

Is it normal for a girl to like being with her girl friends more than with the boys she dates?

Of course. This is true for both boys and girls. Beginning to have relationships with the opposite sex does not mean giving up your friendships with members of your own sex. Girls and boys are often scared by having to spend too much time with each other and need to retreat into the snug harbor of familiar friendships. Girls and boys develop very warm and affectionate feelings toward their friends of the same sex, sharing many experiences, wishes, and hopes together. As you come to feel more comfortable with members of the opposite sex, you will share these good feelings with members of your own sex. Your friendships with people of the same sex will not be given up just because you may like others of the opposite sex more.

Do people who are homosexual or lesbian ever stop being that way?

Some do. When they are unhappy with the way of life such involvements bring, they can change. Usually it takes psychological help, such as from a psychiatrist or psychoanalyst. Others feel very contented and feel no wish to change.

FEELINGS ABOUT YOUR FAMILY

In adolescence your focus is so much on the you in yourself that sometimes it is hard to realize you are living with a bunch of people who are thinking about the them in themselves too! These others are called mothers, fathers, sisters, and brothers—your family. At some point during adolescence you may feel that you and your family are just not getting along as well as you used to. Friends are easier to deal with because usually they too are going through the same intense preoccupation with themselves as you are.

It may seem to you that everything (and sometimes anything) your mother or father may say or do is either wrong, annoying, disrupting, interrupting, cruel, callous, ununderstanding, restricting, dumb, or demanding. Parents, on the other hand, find it hard to adjust to the fact that their sweet youngster is suddenly doing and saying things that seem either wrong, annoying, disrupting, interrupting, cruel, callous, ununderstanding, restricting, dumb, or demanding. Things might get a bit strained at this point.

During adolescence you will change, and this is what can make it a difficult time for parents and their children. When someone changes, others in the relationship have to adjust. And sometimes this is a bumpy procedure for everyone.

Inevitably, in the effort to grow up, some of the ties that bind parent and child must be broken. In order for the child to feel independent, to develop his or her own potentialities and values in life as an adult, he or she must break the bond of extreme closeness that characterized childhood. Younger, dependent children want to do everything their parents do, be wherever their parents are, and act in a manner only suited to bring them their parents' loving smiles. These are some of the kind of bonds that fall by the wayside as adolescents emerge into their own adulthood.

It is sometimes hard, though, not to get these childhood bonds of extreme closeness confused with other kinds of ties that bind—bonds of love or respect or understanding. In the effort to break childhood bonds these ties may be broken too, and this can cause unhappiness. Breaking away from an understanding of your own parents, your need or love of them, and their need of you, is not really growing up at all. Being free, independent, and grown up comes from learning which chains to break. Understanding the many different needs of your own personality will be helpful to you. Trying to understand your parents' personalities will help even more.

Mothers are not just mothers. They are daughters, girls, lovers, wives, friends, and mothers all in one. Fathers, too, are not just fathers but sons, boys, lovers, husbands, and friends too. These are the other parts of your parents' personalities that you can now learn to see and understand as you loosen your hold upon the parent part of their personality. You can help them to see you less as a child if you see them not just as parents but also as people with needs and feelings to be understood by you. This kind of approach will give both of you freedom to change, to adjust, and to grow.

How can I make my parents understand that I am old enough to make my own decisions?

Standing by and letting you practice making foolish decisions (although this is necessary to some extent) makes parents edgy. Try to aim for freedom in certain kinds of decisions first. Show your parents you are indeed ready by trying to use your best judgment when making these decisions. Show your parents, in little ways and big, that they can trust you. This will perhaps allow your parents to feel more comfortable, and as you gain experience, they may allow you greater and greater freedom in making other decisions.

Why do my parents expect me to act as though I'm grown-up and still try to tell me what to do?

Parents have mixed needs and desires, just as you do. They expect you to grow up, on the one hand, and fear that you will, on the other. They may want you to act as a responsible adult but be reluctant to let you take responsibility for your decisions because they still want to protect you from getting hurt. Pointing out this discrepancy may help them stop giving you these double messages. Even if this doesn't work, it will help you understand how they may feel.

How can you be independent and still be expected to do what your parents want you to?

Being independent is not the same as saying no to your parents' wishes. Being independent can also mean that you do something for someone for his or her reasons, even though you may have a personal opinion that differs. If you do only what you want, you are not really independent but isolated and having your own way. Interacting with other people, whether it is your parents or friends, involves compromise and give-and-take, but this does not mean you are lacking independence.

Why is it so hard for my parents to let me grow up?

Parents sometimes find it hard to let go because you are their last family. Once, long ago, they left the homes where they were part of another family. They made a life and family of their own. This family is irreplaceable for them, and you are an important part of it. Some parents base their lives entirely on their children and find it hard to let the ties loosen.

I love my folks, but why don't I want to spend as much time with them as I used to? I'd rather be with my friends.

Loving your parents changes from "I want to be with you all the time, do what you do, and be what you are" to "I love you, but I am a separate person." Drawing away from your family by creating a new family of friends is the normal way adolescents prepare for adulthood, when they will leave their parental home and create a family of their own.

Why does it seem that everything my parents tell me is demanding and unreasonable?

This is a time when you want to begin listening to yourself, doing what you want, when you want, and how you want. Anyone who interferes with this seems to be demanding and unreasonable. In your effort to protect this new selfhood you may lash out and become harsh or impatient with parents. Parents may retaliate, not even being aware of what you are going through, and the merry-go-round has begun. Stopping it will require communication, first with yourself and then with them. Don't expect to do this overnight. Have patience.

Why is it that every time I try to talk to my parents about something, we end up arguing?

There is a difference between discussing something and arguing destructively about it. In arguing, you and your parents are trying to defend opposing positions. You are in a tug-of-war. Who is right? Who is smarter? Who holds the power? Discussing problems means that you try to understand the other side, not just defend your side of things. This constructive approach has no winner but no loser either.

I like myself the way I am, but my parents keep criticizing almost everything I do. What am I supposed to do?

It is difficult to give up what you like about yourself under any conditions, and even harder if you are doing so just to keep the peace and to keep your parents' approval. Talking about your predicament with your parents may help. If they see the dilemma you are in and understand that you want their approval as well as your own, they may be more appreciative of your needs. They may even change their views some of the time. Mostly, parents will understand the need for you to build a good opinion of yourself based upon your choices, not their criticism.

Why does it seem that my parents dislike everything I like?

They are probably wondering why you don't like everything they do. You must be careful to learn which choices are truly yours and which are just born of the need to be different. It may be that you are genuinely evolving into a very unique kind of person, or it may be that in order to feel grown-up, you unconsciously do not want or do not like something just because it is reminiscent of them. Turning your back upon the values your parents hold is not the road to growing up. Picking and choosing your own values, regardless of whether they are the same or different from those of your parents, is more of a direct path.

What do you do if your parents don't seem to like your friends?

If parents don't like any of your friends, perhaps you should take some time out to discover what it is they don't like and why. Sometimes one or two friends may not fit in with their picture of what they want you to be like. This may be a good thing or it could be a bad thing. At this crossroad, it is best to stop and think, and then talk with your parents so they can feel more comfortable with your values and likes. Also you can get to feel more comfortable with their values and dislikes.

When should I be allowed to stay out as late as I want to?

Staying out late is all right if it does not interfere with your health, safety, or school. Add to this the ingredient of your parents' values. If they simply cannot allow anything past a certain hour, then you will have to wait either until you are older or until you can convince them that what you want is reasonable. Also, it may depend upon where you want to stay out late. Overnight at someone's house is one thing; out "on the

streets" is another. If it is someplace your parents do not have
to worry about, the chances are you will be allowed to stay out
later, even if that is not as late as you might want. It is very
important, too, to get home on time after you have been given
the privilege of staying out to a definite hour.

Shouldn't teen-agers be allowed privacy if they want it?

Absolutely. But then, privacy means different things to different people. Privacy can be translated into politeness. Sometimes it takes parents a little while to adjust to the fact that
their child is becoming a person in his or her own right and has
a right to privacy.

*I used to play a lot with my sister, but she just seems so young
and silly to me now. The family is mad at me because I ignore
her. What am I supposed to do?*

You don't have to play with your sister, but perhaps if you
would not ignore her, it would be better. Sometimes just being
kind or saying something nice to a kid sister counts for hours of
playing.

*Should you have to share a room with your brother if you are a
girl?*

No. And brothers should not have to share a room with a sister
either, unless family finances are such that there is no other
choice. Brothers and sisters, after the very young childhood
years, are best off in separate rooms. The natural evolution of
sexuality in females and males makes it a strained situation
for both sexes. It is normal to feel this way, even if it is as close a
relation as a brother or a sister.

*Why don't I care about keeping my things as neat and clean as
my mother wants me to?*

As a young child, you were used to your mother taking care of your things for you. She had all the responsibility. Now you have to take some of the responsibility yourself. When the responsibility for your things, your clothes, your room, and so on is entirely yours, you may find you care more about it. But it is hard to give up the feeling of wanting to be taken care of.

Why is it sometimes so hard to tell my parents the truth?

Taking the consequences of telling the truth may be very difficult. The consequences may be very harsh, or they may simply be your own fear of what your parents will think. Most people do not like to risk the displeasure of their parents, and telling the truth runs this risk. It may be easier if you recognize that much of the time parents appreciate the fact that you were straight with them, no matter what the truth may be.

Sometimes I don't want to go places with my parents. Why should I have to go?

Parents may reasonably expect you to do something just for them. They like to be with you, and they know that their time with you is limited. Even though at times they may argue or get angry, they still want the family feeling of togetherness that your presence provides.

FEELINGS ABOUT YOURSELF

For most people, all kinds of feelings during adolescence become very intense. Not the least of these are the feelings you may have with regard to yourself. Your mental image of the kind of person you are becoming may at times be a very confusing or distressing one. There are so many changes taking place in you, physically and emotionally, that it is sometimes hard to keep track of them yourself.

Sometimes you may feel very much like a young adult capable of anything, and the next moment, very much like a young child capable of nothing. These feelings of omnipotence and helplessness are not unusual in adolescence or even later on in adulthood. Being an adolescent does not begin or end abruptly overnight. Childhood and some of the feelings of childhood represent a part of your life that is never really over. There is a child in each of us forever. Sometimes, just when you feel really grown up at last, you may come across some of the child in yourself and feel that all your new, more adult capability is gone. It is not, of course; it is simply being woven into the cloth of your personality, a fabric made up of childhood threads as well.

Feelings about yourself, especially the way you look, can become a mixture of pride and agonizing self-criticism. Your perception of the way you are and your desire to be something else may lead to all sorts of worries—worry about being too tall or too short, too big or too small, too wide or too narrow, too nice or too mean, too shy or too aggressive, too smart or too dumb. In short, you may begin to feel that your body or your personality is just not turning out the way you wished or expected it would. On top of this, you may feel that everyone else seems to be doing just fine! But it really is not that way at all. There is no perfect way to look or to be.

Feelings about yourself in relation to others of your age can suddenly become very important. Just as you are really beginning to look and feel different, you may want more than anything else to be, or to look, just as you imagine everyone else does. But no two people go through adolescence at exactly the same time or in exactly the same way. When you were young children, you were not so much aware of the differences between yourself and other children. Everyone seemed to lose their two front teeth at just about the same time! Puberty changes all that.

The infinite variations that make each adult look, act, and feel unique begin to show up during adolescence. It feels strange and unfamiliar to be different, even in small ways, and causes the longing to be once again "just like everyone else," the way it used to be.

What can I do if I don't like the way I look?

This will depend upon what you don't like about your looks. Hair can be made to grow longer or shorter, curlier or straighter. Teeth can be fixed, posture improved, weight can be lost or gained. The point is that some things can be changed for the better. Even personality traits can be worked on. Find the specific thing you wish were better and work on it. If it cannot be made better, then you have to learn to live with it, and chances are, you may even grow to love it! You not only have the power to change your looks or traits but the power to like yourself more.

What should I do if others don't like the things I like about myself?

This is one of the paths of adolescence that require delicate navigation. You are discovering who you are and what you are. Your tastes, preferences, and style are all being shaped. The opinions of those around you have great influence. When opinions sharply differ, some adjustments may be in order. These do not necessarily have to be your adjustments. After you evaluate what you like and find it genuine, keep it. Eventually others will be able to appreciate it also.

Why do I feel so shy around people?

Many people feel the same way. Adolescence has often been called the awkward age. Adolescents may sometimes wish to hide and avoid the risk of exposure and potential criticism. Your own estimation of yourself and the way you size up to your own ideal may have left you feeling less than perfect. The reality is that others do not see you with the same harshness you see yourself. Try not being so shy with other people. Although at first you may still feel the same, gradually your feelings of being shy will change.

How can I be more self-confident?

Self-confidence will not descend upon you automatically. You have to work for it by struggling with your anxieties. Self-confidence is built by success, the small kind of success of a personal nature, not the gigantic, awe-inspiring success that the world bestows upon you. The first step is to establish a plan, a plan called ACT. *A* stands for *assessment.* Assess the reality of your positive achievements, no matter how insignificant they may seem. Do not dwell upon your fears, your shortcomings, your "wish I were." *C* stands for *confront.* Confront yourself with the emotional issues that bother you. Chart yourself a course, in whatever direction you wish to go. Now let the *A* and *C* transform themselves into action. Try—this is the *T*. Struggle with your anxieties and take the first step toward whatever you want to be or wherever you want to go. No matter how the struggle turns out, you can take much pride in your effort. Trying is in itself a success.

Why do I feel so lonely?

Adolescence is an in-between time for people. This is the time when you begin to detach yourself from an emotionally intimate and dependent relationship with your parents. Because parents no longer fulfill all of your emotional needs for love, approval, and companionship, there will be a gap in your life. Friends can help fill the gap, but friends go home, move away, or stop being friends, and loneliness returns. Adolescence can be a very lonely time until you can share your life with a loved one.

Why do my feelings always seem to be getting hurt?

During adolescence, feelings are very easily hurt, since everything is up for grabs. Everything can hang on a smile, a frown, a word, or lack of a word. The reason is that your self-esteem is being built. Until you have more time for good experiences to build a healthy sense of self-worth, you are very dependent upon what others say about you, think about you, and feel about you. Any lack of approval, any rejection—real or imagined—can easily hurt you.

How come I feel I like my friends more than they like me?

Some friends can be jealous, fickle, and even mean. If these are the kind of people you like, stop and think why! Good friends may really like you, and yet you may feel they do not. As you become more sure that you are worth liking, you will become more confident that people like you.

Why is it hard for me to make friends?

Making friends requires that you extend yourself to someone. This is hard to do because you become vulnerable to their rejection; perhaps they will show they do not care for you as much as you care for them. Friendship involves two persons being open and trusting. Trying to make friends, even though it may not always work out, may reward you with a close, warm friendship. Just one real friend can mean a great deal.

Sometimes I get so mad I just don't know what to do.

Learning how to deal with love is one difficult part of life, and learning how to deal with hate and anger is the other. During adolescence you become aware of your power to hurt— emotionally and physically—if you choose. Controlling your rage, coupled with your growing awareness of your own power, is very hard to do and takes time. This does not mean that anger should be repressed. Try to understand the reasons for your anger, try to talk about it, and learn to channel it in a good direction.

What good does it do to talk about your problems or feelings?

Basically, honest, open communication gives each person the opportunity to try to learn how to make the other person happy.

It feels less lonely and isolating when you can talk to someone about the things that disturb you. Talking to yourself can be very helpful too. Some adolescents find that writing their thoughts down in a diary provides them with the same good feeling they get when confiding in a very good friend.

Why do I care about not being liked?

When others do not like you, you may not like yourself. During adolescence this kind of dependence upon outside approval from friends is very common. As you grow up, you will be less dependent upon what others think of you. During adolescence feelings of self-worth can change rapidly. One moment you have them, the next they are gone. If a good friend does not like you any longer or a group of friends do not want to include you, it can have a devastating impact. Some adolescents are ready to try anything in order to get approval. Taking dope or drinking too much are examples of extreme and misguided efforts to obtain approval. You need courage to face feeling not liked. Having this courage will help you like yourself more and need this kind of approval less!

Why am I sometimes so embarrassed by my parents? They really bug me.

As a normal part of the process of separation, adolescents may begin to notice things wrong with their once-perfect parents. An accent, lack of knowledge, style of clothes, hair, shoes, values—everything—comes under new and careful scrutiny. Feeling guilty about this only buries these feelings, temporarily. Trying to be fair, despite these feelings, is probably easier on all of you.

Why am I so embarrassed about my parents being divorced?

Children of divorce often feel as though they have done something shameful or wrong, something that has made them so unlovable that a parent leaves. In the fantasy of childhood, parents never leave if they love you. In reality, parents who divorce do not leave you. Parents do not divorce children, they separate from their adult mate. Also, they will continue to be your parent and love you as long as they live, no matter where they live.

AFTERWORD

Sometimes the feelings and events which occur during adolescence can seem overwhelming. But you need not feel helpless or powerless. For adolescence holds a promise for you—the promise of discovery. By the end of your adolescent years, you will have discovered the power of your emerging self. You will feel your power most when you are successful and least when beset by inner doubt and fear. But from adolescence on, your personal power will be there all the time. Use it well.

INDEX

Abortion, 83-86
Acne (pimples), 27, 36
Advances by boys, 95
Anesthesia
  in abortion, 84-85
  in childbirth, 69, 70, 72
Anger, 112
Athletic boys, 37

Babies
  birth of, see Childbirth
  desire for, 75
  nursing of, 74-75
  premature, 73
Baldness, 36
Beard, 31, 35-36
Birth control, 77-83
Birth control clinics, 81, 82, 86
Body hair at puberty, 11, 29-31
Brassieres, 19, 20
Breasts
  in pregnancy, 74-75
  at puberty, 11, 17-20
Breech babies, 74
Brothers and sisters, 107

Caesarian section, 72-73
Cervix, 13, 66
  in abortion, 85
Childbirth, 65-76
  appearance of baby at,
    75-76
  Caesarian section in,
    72-73
  death during, 70, 72

fathers at, 70-72
feet-first babies in, 74
mother's body after, 74
natural, 69-70
timing of, 73
Circumcision, 34
Conception, 57-62
Clitoris, 12
  compared to penis, 14
  in sexual intercourse, 54-55
"Come," meaning of, 39
Communication
  about feelings, 112-13
  on sexual intercourse, 81
Condom (rubber, 77-79, 89
Cream, spermicidal, 78

Dating, 91-96
  asking by girls, 92
Diaphragm, 78, 80-82
Divorced parents, 113-14
Double standard, 97
Douches, 27, 79
Drugstores, birth-control devices
  in, 81-82

Egg (ovum), 13, 21-23
  in conception, 57-62
Ejaculations, 30, 38-44, 60
  number of, 43
  See also Orgasms
Embyro, see Fetus
Episiotomy, 69
Erections, 38-44
  uncontrollable, 42

Fallopian tubes, 13-14, 15, 21, 57
Family, feelings about, 102-5, 113-14
Fathers
  boys' ability to become, 30, 41
  at childbirth, 70-72
  See also Parents
Feminine, meaning of, 16
Fetus, 62-66
  in abortion, 85
  sex of, 62
Figure development in girls, 19-20
First base, 94
Flirting, 95
Foam, spermicidal, 78
Foreskin, 34
French kiss, 94
Friends, 112
  parents and, 104-6
  same-sex, 101

Going all the way, 97, 99
Going steady, 95
Gonorrhea, 87
Growth, physical, 11, 16, 17, 31-34
Guilt
  about ejaculations, 43
  about masturbation, 48-51
  about sexual fantasies, 46

Hate, 112
Height, 11, 16, 31-33
Herpes genitalis, 87
Homosexuality, 99-102
Hospital, childbirth at, 70-72
Hymen, 13, 53

Intercourse, *see* Sexual intercourse
IUD (intrauterine device), 78, 81

Jealousy, 96
Jelly, spermicidal, 78

Kissing
  on dates, 92-93, 94

French, 94
  pregnancy and, 60
  VD and, 88
Kotex, 28

Labia, 13
Labor, 69-72
Larynx, boys', 36
Lesbians, 100-2
Loneliness, 111
Looks, 110
Love
  for babies, 75
  dating and, 91, 96
  for parents, 102-4
  sex compared to, 98
  sexual intercourse and, 51, 53-54, 56, 77
  women's attitudes to, 97

Making out, 93-96
Masculine, meaning of, 38
Masturbation, 45-51, 54
  guilt and embarrassment about, 48-51
  myths about, 49
Menopause, 28
Menstruation, 21-25
  age at, 23-24
  length of period, 25-26, 28
  as natural function, 24-25
  the pill and, 80
  pregnancy and, 23, 27, 57
  sexual organs during, 13, 21-23
Modess, 28
Modesty, 20-21
Muscles, 37

Necking, 93-96
Nipples, 17-19
Nursing, 74-75

Orgasms, 45-52
  boys' vs. girls' compared, 48
  description of, 47

length of, 47
in masturbation, 48, 50
pregnancy and, 60
in sexual intercourse, 52, 54
Ovaries, 13, 15, 21, 57
Ovum, *see* Egg

Parents, feelings about, 102-8, 113-14
Penis, 29-31, 33-35
erections of, 38-44
in sexual intercourse, 52-53
size of, 33-34, 39
Petting, 93-96
Pill, the 78, 79-80, 82
Pimples, 27, 26
Pituitary gland, 24
Placenta, 62, 64, 66, 70
Planned Parenthood, 82, 86
Pregnancy, 57-65
boys' ejaculations and, 41
fetus in, 62-66
how to tell, 61
menstruation and, 23, 27
number of times of sexual intercourse needed for, 81
sex of baby in, 61
sexual organs, during, 13, 15
See also Abortion; Childbirth
Premature babies, 73
Privacy, 107
Prostate gland, 29, 38
Puberty
in boys, 29-37
feelings during, 90-91, 105-14
in girls, 11, 16-21
Pubic hair, 15, 29-30

Rectal opening, 13
Rhythm method, 82-83
Rubber, 77-79, 89

Sanitary napkins, 26, 28
internal, 27, 28
Scrotum, 29

Second base, 94
Self-confidence, 111
Semen (seminal fluid), 38, 39, 42, 60
Sexual experimentation, 98
Sexual fantasies, 46-48
Sexual intercourse, 51-56
done by almost everybody, 99
enjoyment of, 55-56
first, 53
frequency of, 56
length of time for, 54
masturbation compared to, 50
old people and, 56
as only means of pregnancy, 60
physical description of, 51-52
size of penis and, 34
sperm in, 39, 40
talking about it first, 81
as victory for boy, 97
See also Birth control
Sexual organs
male, 26-35
female, 11-15
Sexual standards of boys vs girls, 97-98
Shaving, 35
Shyness, 110
Sperm, 30, 38-42
in conception, 57-61
Spermicidal foam, 78, 81
Staying out late, 106-7
Swimming during menstruation, 27
Syphilis, 87

Tampons, 27, 28
Teasing by girls, 97
Telling about sexual experiences, 99
Testicles, 29-31, 33, 38, 39, 44
Third base, 94
Twins, 61, 73-74

Umbilical cord, 62, 66

Urethra, 12, 42
Urination
  by boys, 38, 42
  by fetuses, 64
  by girls, 12
Uterus, 13, 15, 21-23, 74
  fetus in, 62-66, 68

Vagina, 13, 14-15

in childbirth, 66, 69, 71, 74
in sexual intercourse, 52, 53
Vasectomy, 79
Venereal disease (VD), 86-89
Virgin, definition of, 52
Voice, boys', change of, 30-31, 36

Wet dreams, 43-44